MONEY

with

Meaning

MONEY

with

Meaning

HOW TO
CREATE JOY AND
IMPACT THROUGH
PHILANTHROPY

ALEX JOHNSTON

LIONCREST
PUBLISHING

MONEY WITH MEANING

How to Create Joy and Impact through Philanthropy

FIRST EDITION

ISBN 978-1-5445-4041-2 *Hardcover*
      978-1-5445-4042-9 *Paperback*
      978-1-5445-4043-6 *Ebook*

For Caroline, Henry, Hugh, and Charles

CONTENTS

INTRODUCTION

*It's Time to Fix Philanthropy—
and Change the World for Real*

On May 25, 2019, novelist and philanthropist MacKenzie Scott signed the Giving Pledge wherein she committed to give away the vast majority of her then $60 billion fortune within her own lifetime. And give she has. In 2020 alone, she gave away $5.7 billion through a simple, trust-based process with almost none of the process-driven trappings of traditional philanthropy. This was more than three times as much as any other donor on that list and was also the largest amount ever given in a single year by any Giving Pledge signer. In fact, since 2010, fifty-one of the sixty-two US-based billionaires who originally signed the Giving Pledge have become wealthier since they signed it. With accelerating wealth creation generally outpacing increases in giving, fewer than ten are actually on track to fulfill their commitment to give away at least half their wealth in their own lifetime.[1]

These statistics are part of the reason so many people, including many of the wealthy themselves, have become so disillusioned with philanthropy. Wealth is ever more concentrated, and the world is on fire with problems more complex and challenging than ever. In spite of all this, most philanthropy still clings to traditional ways and operates without a sense of urgency. MacKenzie Scott's dramatically divergent example only seems to underscore this point. The world is in need of thoughtful, committed philanthropists now more than ever, and still there are billions and billions of dollars sitting on the sidelines.

Despite the rising critique of philanthropy, there are many engaged, successful donors, including some working below the radar. They are making concrete progress on some of the toughest challenges imperiling our shared future. Take, for example, Liz Thompson, who, along with her husband, Don, founded the Cleveland Avenue Foundation for Education. She is working to address poverty in the US with a strategy grounded in her own experience as a Black woman growing up in Chicago's Cabrini Green neighborhood. She is also working to engage fellow philanthropists with the 1954 Project, creating a space where philanthropists of color can come together around a similar grantmaking strategy on a larger scale. Or consider Sharon Chang, a successful entertainment-industry entrepreneur who has founded the Guild of Future Architects. The Guild convenes a wide variety of stakeholders and uses design thinking principles to develop solutions for challenges from climate change to the spread of misinformation online.

Another example is Katherine Bradley and her innovative, tireless, twenty-plus-year commitment to advancing public education in Washington, DC. She has played a key role in helping DC mayors and superintendents implement powerful reforms. These changes have resulted in DC students making some of the most striking academic improvements in the country. Yet another example is Dustin Moskowitz and Cari Tuna. They have centered their giving around a commitment to maximizing human welfare through an approach known as "effective altruism." Along the way they have helped build a whole field of supportive infrastructure other donors can draw upon.

I hope you are reading this book because you're in a position to be part of the change so desperately needed in philanthropy. If you are financially capable of giving away tens of millions, hundreds of millions, or even billions of dollars in your lifetime and want to know how to truly, genuinely *help* people and the planet with that money, this book is for you. If you are a trusted advisor working with donors like this, you'll find value here as well. And even if you don't have this scale of money at your disposal, my hope is that any donor with the aspiration to make the world a better place will also find value in the tools, frameworks, and perspectives in this book.

So, if you're thinking about giving more and giving better, how do you go about it? What knowledge, skills, and mindsets do you need to cultivate to maximize your own potential as a philanthropist? What does it take to gear up your giving in a way that creates both joy and impact for the world and for you as a donor?

As so many aspiring philanthropists know, it can be very easy to get stuck as you try to make the most of your giving. Whether or not the larger world knows or sympathizes, there are real obstacles that stand in the way of high-capacity donors.

But here's the good news: although the obstacles facing you as a donor are real, it's not actually as hard as it might seem to move past them. The trick is understanding that the knowledge, skills, and mindsets that have served you so well in other areas of your life may not produce the results you expect when it comes to your giving. Some of the moves for finding more impact and more joy through philanthropy can seem counterintuitive. In some cases you will need to make subtle but profound shifts in thinking. That's why so many people with the opportunity to create deep meaning with their money are missing out by giving up on giving. Don't fall into the trap of leaving your money on the sidelines in a world where so many compelling needs abound and philanthropy still has a vital role to play.

Meaningful giving begins with being willing to learn and to develop yourself as a donor and a human being. This journey is worth it. Getting your giving right can truly change the world for real, and it can be one of the most powerful sources of meaning and joy in your life as well.

How do I know? I am the president and founder of Building Impact, a firm specializing in philanthropic advising. Over the past decade, our firm has helped clients give away over $750 million. Nonetheless, in this book I am not speaking for these clients or for my partners and colleagues at Building Impact. The ideas here reflect my own perspective on creating joy and impact through philanthropy. I have gained an additional vantage point on the challenges of translating money into meaning by helping to found and lead a nonprofit advocacy organization for seven years. I am also a member of the Entrepreneurs Organization and serve as an advisor and board member for several entrepreneurial nonprofits.

My outlook is also shaped by my own voyage of personal and professional growth. Over the past five years, my desire to feel a deeper sense of alignment and joy across all the areas of my life has led me to delve deeply at the intersection of personal development, philanthropy, and social change. Through extensive reading and study as well as the completion of more than twenty specific trainings, I have gained powerful insights in my own journey. What I have learned has inspired me to help others on a similar path. I am a Certified High Performance Coach and have worked with dozens of donors, advisors, and social entrepreneurs. All are forging their own paths of personal and professional growth as people with a calling to contribute to a better world.

Along the way, I have also held leadership roles in the public sector, from director of operations at a housing authority to school board member. And at the center of it all, I am a husband and the father of three boys.

As mentioned, I have spent the last decade working as an advisor to philanthropists who have confronted (and in many cases, overcome) all kinds of obstacles. So, let's talk a little more about what impedes successful philanthropy. First of all, gearing up your giving is not just a question of how much money you have to give—there's also the question of how much time and energy you're prepared to spend doing it. Perhaps you feel like giving well will take more time, energy, and specialized knowledge than you have. Due to this, you may be looking for someone who has the time and expertise to oversee these efforts on your behalf. Unfortunately, it can seem prohibitively hard to find someone you really trust who is also good at this job and who *also* shares your vision.

Then there are all the structure and design questions—do you tackle these before you find help or after? Not every philanthropist hits the ground running with a working knowledge of whether they need to set up an LLC, DAF, or private foundation to ensure proper allocation of resources. Or would it be better to just stick with writing checks, no matter how big they get? And what if the advice you get initially from tax and financial planning professionals ends up locking you into structures that don't actually serve your philanthropic aims as they evolve?

Whether or not you have a trusted advisor at your side, it can still be overwhelming when people and organizations who've caught wind of your giving begin asking you for money. You can quickly find yourself stuck in a web of social obligations that spread your giving too thin to make a real difference on the issues you care most about. It may be tempting to stop discussing philanthropy altogether to avoid being pulled into further causes. Even if you do manage to focus your giving on the issues you care most about, it can be remarkably hard to feel sure your dollars are actually making a difference—especially if you are committed to tackling the kind of complex challenges that matter most to our shared future.

If you've felt any of these things, the first thing to know is that you are not alone! I can tell you that many donors are wrestling with these very same obstacles. Whatever the scale of resources you have to give away, this book is here to help you work through the issues impeding your impact and your satisfaction as a donor. In addition to providing answers for all the aforementioned issues, I will cover the ins and outs of seven different legal structures for carrying out your giving. This book will also describe how to avoid the pitfalls of selfish, senseless, and spiritless giving so your philanthropic efforts truly make the world a better place and leave you feeling fulfilled. You have the power to make a real and measurable impact on the causes you care about—and to feel a deep sense of joy as you do so!

This book distills years of trial and error as well as practical learning, all synthesized from working with dozens of philanthropists and scores of social entrepreneurs. It is designed to make it much easier, more joyful, and more impactful for busy, well-meaning people who want to accomplish even more in their philanthropic mission. This is what I try to do for the philanthropists I coach individually. Whether you want to spend an hour a month on your giving or fifty hours a week, the idea is to save you lots of time and energy by creating a curated collection of resources and learning. That's why this book comes with a supplemental set of worksheets, instructional videos, and other resources if you want to dig deeper on any particular point. You can find this material on this book's website, www.moneywithmeaningbook.co.

This book is not a condemnation of philanthropy. A quick tour of the bestseller lists shows that this has become a popular sport. But just as Winston Churchill once quipped, "Democracy is the worst form of government, except for all the others," so, too, with philanthropy. Despite all its challenges and potential shortcomings, I believe that philanthropy done well is vital for our political and social lives to function as they should.

This book brings together key insights from different fields in a way you won't find anywhere else. It's a practical and carefully curated tool kit for philanthropists who want to answer the call to make the most of themselves as servants of a higher good. You can enjoy life-changing results from this book, *but only if you take action to implement what you learn here into the structure and process of your giving and your daily life.*

HOW TO USE THIS BOOK

There are many paths you can take through this book. The most obvious one is to read it straight through, as the chapters are set up to progress through key stages of learning and growth as a donor. The book is also accessible as a reference guide that you can jump into at any point where your interest is greatest. If you want to start at the beginning, the first few chapters are all about taking stock, setting a vision, and figuring out what really matters most in your giving. If the prospect of leaning into your giving feels like an uninspiring chore, Chapter 4 gives you six straightforward alternatives to the conventional path of strategic philanthropy, and Chapter 5 offers five big ideas for creating outsize impact at whatever level of resources you're starting with. If you feel like you have some pressing choices to make about which legal and organizational vehicles to use, Chapter 6 walks you through the seven leading options for structuring your giving. If you're drawn to work on the toughest challenges and you want to really pressure-test your ideas, Chapter 7 gives you a practical guide to apply the tools of systems thinking, critical thinking, and design thinking to complex philanthropic endeavors. If you're grappling with how to know if your money is really making a difference, Chapter 8 is all about assessing the impact of your giving. If your key concern is acquiring help and working effectively with others to carry out your giving, you'll find that in Chapters 9 and 10. And finally, if the thought of gearing up your giving keeps looping back to hesitations you may have about pushing past your comfort zone, you can jump right to Chapters 11 and 12. They are all about your personal development as a donor.

No matter where you start in this book—no matter where you are in your journey to translate money into meaning—it all comes back to this: are you ready to learn and grow in pursuit of more joy and more impact in your giving? And here's a bonus: by doing so, you'll actually be helping to fix what ails philanthropy while you're at it!

Keep reading because it's time to change the world *for real*.

TAKING STOCK

How Meaningful Is Your Giving?

> *"The meaning of life is to find your gift.*
> *The purpose of life is to give it away."*
>
> —Pablo Picasso

As you look to gear up your giving, the very first thing to do is take stock with two simple questions:

How much impact do you think you are having?

How much satisfaction are you feeling?

These two questions go hand in hand, but too often philanthropists focus more on one than the other. Let's explore this further with a four-question self-assessment.

1. Have you ever engaged in giving that you knew wasn't helping those in the greatest need but was super important to you personally? Maybe you supported an educational institution your children attend or the

capital campaign for someplace that already has a huge endowment.

2. Have you ever engaged in giving that you were pretty sure wasn't producing much benefit for others and didn't bring you much satisfaction either? Maybe this was giving that you were doing to satisfy a social obligation, or it was the pet project of another branch of the family. Or, maybe you've had the experience of giving money to a donor-advised fund but haven't gotten around to putting the money to work in the world by making distributions.

3. Have you ever pushed so hard to maximize the impact of your giving that you squeezed the joy out of it with performance contracts, metrics, and milestones—and *still* came away wondering if you were actually achieving the impact you were hoping for?

4. How often have you hit the sweet spot in your giving, such as grants that truly support people and organizations you really believe are making a difference in the world? How often do these successes bring you a deep sense of personal fulfillment and satisfaction?

If you consider your present situation, what's the relative balance for you between these four types of giving? There's no judgment here—this is just a conversation you're having with yourself. To get even more clarity about your experience so far, if you were to assign a ten-point scale to the positive social impact of your giving to date, how would you rate your giving overall?

And what about your overall sense of satisfaction and personal fulfillment? You should have two numbers now, even if they are the same number. Now, let's plot these as (x, y) coordinates on the chart below:

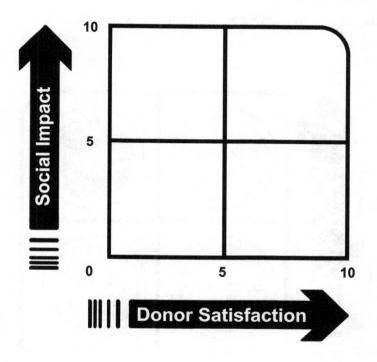

Which quadrant do you fall in today?

As we delve into a more detailed review of the kind of giving that occurs in each quadrant, you may gain insight into why you might be feeling turned off by a lot of what you see going on in the world of philanthropy. Most importantly, I hope this will help you reflect on where you are currently and where you want to end up.

THE MIND *AND* MATTER FRAMEWORK:
FOUR KINDS OF GIVING

For simplicity's sake, I've divided giving into four categories: selfish, senseless, spiritless, and meaningful. Let's start by filling in the same chart from before with more information, as illustrated below.

Only one of these four boxes is a place you want to end up as you gear up your giving: meaningful giving. Let's walk through each to see why.

Selfish Giving

This is what happens when a donor focuses on gratifying their own immediate, ego-driven needs without much regard for the greater good. This might involve giving money to an already-wealthy private school or having a building named after you to better ensure your kids will get through the admissions process. Often, selfish giving is more like a purchase disguised as philanthropy. There are other forms of self-centered giving that aren't quite so blatant. For example, when a donor is so attached to their own vision of making change and how the world works that they execute their giving in a way that builds up a bubble of BS all around them. Their grantees and staff are all whitewashing reality to fit within the storyline this type of giver insists is true, regardless of contradictory evidence from the real world.

Senseless Giving

Next, let's talk about senseless giving. This is the kind of giving that doesn't produce significant social impact or satisfaction to the donor. What? Why would someone do this? Because, in a number of cases, people use their giving to meet relatively trivial needs. A good example of this is a social obligation: you came to my dinner party, so I'll buy a table at your charity gala. In this instance, the giving is more of a friendly trade and has little to do with what the cause is or even whether the recipient is doing something that actually benefits others. There are too many nonprofit organizations whose true reason for being is more about sustaining a set of social connections under the guise of "purpose" than advancing a mission of significant social consequence. There's nothing wrong with this per se, but we shouldn't confuse this kind of activity with making the world a better place. Sometimes the self-serving and the senseless intersect. Reflexive, reciprocal giving to someone else's self-serving philanthropic project is a great example of this. Think about people who have given to Donald Trump's "charities" only to end up subsidizing the painting of his personal portraits that hang in the clubhouses of his golf courses.

Of course, there's another form of senseless giving that is perhaps the most senseless of all: parking huge amounts of money in donor-advised funds without actually giving it away. Technically, this is "giving" because in a formal, legal sense, the donor no longer owns these assets and has received the benefit of a charitable tax deduction. In reality, this money is sitting on the sidelines, not producing any impact. Meanwhile, the world is on fire. What is more senseless than that?

Spiritless Giving

What is spiritless giving? This is about seeking maximum social impact in a joyless, nonrelational, untrusting, mechanistic way. We see examples of this in grant agreements that are hyperfocused on metrics and milestones regardless of whether they truly serve the intended impact. The metaphor here is important. "Milestones" imply that we are on a road going from one clear destination to another. We can measure exactly how much progress we've made with reference to these markers. How well do you think that metaphor holds up to the actual reality of making progress against complex social challenges? A related indicator of spiritless giving is focusing on verification and documentation of every little detail that is susceptible to empirical analysis. This loses focus on the big picture and is deeply dispiriting for nonprofit, social entrepreneurs who have proximity to the issues they are working on. They know if they could just do what made sense on the ground, they would be able to achieve far more impact than by dutifully following rigidly structured grant agreements.

So, what's going on here? How do donors get caught in this trap of confusing rigor for relevance? One of the most common reasons is that they are conducting their giving from a place of distrust. This can easily happen if your mental model of human nature tells you that left to their own devices, most people will goof off and take advantage. From this perspective, the vision and drive in your giving has to come from you and you alone. Grantees are "hired help" on whom you have to keep a watchful eye. Another reason some donors fall into spiritless giving is confusion—even fear—in the face of uncertainty about how their philanthropic "investments" are performing. These donors don't deliberately want to run roughshod over their grantees, but they also have no idea how to tell if their precious resources are actually producing the results they want to achieve. So, they go overboard measuring whatever they can and hope for the best, or they shift their investments only to what is easily measurable at the expense of what is more meaningful.

For all these reasons, spiritless giving is not a stable equilibrium for most donors. It's often a slippery slope toward senseless giving: giving less or not at all because the experience feels so frustrating and joyless. This brings us to the idea of "currency of fulfillment." Only when you are feeling sufficiently fulfilled by your giving will you stick with it and truly maximize your positive impact and potential as a philanthropist.

Meaningful Giving

The good news is there is a better way. Meaningful giving is where social impact and donor satisfaction are integrated into something greater. This is giving in which the donor pursues a personally meaningful vision for a better world, while at the same time embracing reality and seeking to understand and learn from those their giving touches. This approach opens up space for the wisdom, passion, and proximity of others to shape the path of your giving. This way of giving is grounded in a respect for the agency of everyone involved and provides a rich context for your own learning and growth as a human being and as a philanthropist. This is the path of joyful impact. We'll spend the rest of this book helping you figure out how to truly *give* in a way that creates meaning for you and the world you live in.

HOW TO CREATE MEANING WITH YOUR MONEY:
THE FOUR FOUNDATIONS OF IMPACT
AND JOY FOR DONORS

So here it is—the most important thing I've learned from a decade of working with donors.

There are four key things you need to focus on to gear up your giving in a way that creates impact, joy, and meaning for you and the world at large. Philanthropy at its best is about *getting visionary, getting real, getting together,* and *getting better.*

Here's a graphic I like to use to illustrate this:

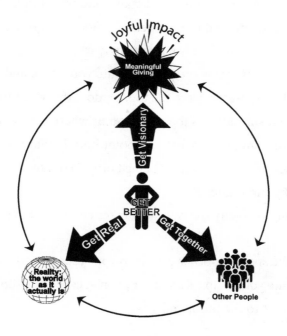

Getting Visionary:
Commit to Prioritizing Visionary Social Impact
Above Ego-Driven Needs

Getting visionary is about creating a vision that is big enough to actually make a difference on the issues that matter, whatever level of resources you are bringing to bear. Great visions are engines, not anchors. You want a vision that pulls you forward, not one that holds you back. This is especially true in philanthropy where it is so easy for donors to dwell on the vision at the expense of actually making progress.

Is the vision for your giving sufficiently vivid *and* grounded in reality to inspire you and others to take action and go after it? A great metaphor for this is a distant mountain range. Imagine looking at its many different peaks. Standing right here, from miles away, do you already know exactly which peak you want to summit? Do you know the precise route you'll take and why it's going to be so great to get to the top? Or does the whole mountain range seem shrouded in fog to the point where you're not even sure there's anything there? The point here is that your philanthropic vision can suffer from being both too rigidly detailed and too murky and vague.

Getting visionary the right way takes an integrated balance:

- Make space for other people in your vision—indeed, create your vision *with* other people, especially those closest to the problem.

- Think big enough to actually solve the problem, even if that means acknowledging that your resources are insufficient on their own.
- Think granular too: figure out what it will take to actually carry out your vision in the real world.
- Identify and account for your own blind spots, cognitive biases, and psychological wiring.
- Embrace complexity and the dimension of time. Look for the unexpected and the interconnected, and appreciate how things may play out over time.
- Be adaptive in your vision—it has to be big, flexible, and inclusive.

This is the kind of blend that makes a vision both inspirational and enduring. This is what it takes to face all the twists and turns that inevitably arise on the journey toward addressing the biggest challenges imperiling our world today.

Getting Real: Seek and Speak the Truth to Everyone, Including Yourself

This is where the rubber hits the road. Can you hold onto that compelling vision while you also confront the messy, disappointing, and even depressing reality of the world? So much philanthropy falls apart when it comes up against the rigors of the real world. Developing an exciting and inspiring vision is often the fun part for donors seeking to translate their money into meaning—even with all the provisos attached to getting your vision right. Facing the harsh reality of the world as it actually is—that's another matter. For many high-capacity donors, dealing with reality is brushed aside as an optional exercise. It's all too easy to surround yourself with a team that will tell you the world is flat if that's what your vision statement and theory of change stipulates. Getting real takes courage, humility, and proximity to the people and places that are most closely involved with the issues you are trying to address.

Getting Together: Treat Others with Consideration, Not Contempt

This is all about working with other people in a connected and effective way. Unfortunately, this is an area where plenty of philanthropy falls drastically short.

A key commitment for meaningful giving is to treat others with consideration, not contempt. "Contempt" is a strong word, but when we engage others as instruments for meeting our own needs and not as agents whose autonomy we respect, we are treating them with a form of contempt. There's a lot more to say about how we can show up in a different way in our relationships with others, and we will explore those frameworks and tools in Chapter 10. For now, it's important to understand that being genuinely open to the influence of others is a foundation for experiencing both more joy and more impact in your giving. Far too often, philanthropists go out in the world looking to enlist others in service of their own vision. It is more effective to begin with deep listening and an openness to supporting the ideas of others.

MacKenzie Scott's approach to philanthropy demonstrates her understanding of the value behind *getting together* in a considerate, collaborative way. First, she identified several key areas that she wanted to make a difference in. Then, she and her team of advisors looked for leaders and organizations who were already out there doing great work or who were still in startup mode but putting together compelling plans. After a very streamlined diligence process, she backed up a metaphorical truck and dumped out the money—no strings attached, no program metrics, milestones, or detailed reporting requirements. This is a radical approach in the world of philanthropy: for her, *not* requiring an ongoing relationship with her grantees represents her way of respecting their ideas and their agency. That said, this is certainly not the only way to create meaning with your money—stay tuned for more ways to do your giving differently in Chapters 4 and 5.

Getting Better: Commit to the Daily Pursuit of Personal Development, Learning, and Growth

Now we get to the part where all this talk about "making the world a better place" comes full circle: back to making yourself into a better *you*. When coaching philanthropists as well as the social entrepreneurs in our accelerator programs, I often say the journey of joyful impact is about making yourself into a more effective instrument of impact and a more expansive vessel of joy. Chapter 12 frames this journey of personal growth around the Seven Pillars of Personal Development. The truth is, you can't *get visionary, get real,* and *get together* in the way we're talking about without also making the commitment to *get better* through the daily pursuit of personal growth and joy across all areas of your life.

DONOR PSYCHOLOGY AND YOU

What Do You Really Need to Get from Your Giving?

> *"It is amazing what you can accomplish if you do not care who gets the credit."*
>
> —HARRY S. TRUMAN

Here's a truth that derails many donors from their pursuit of meaningful giving: there's a part of all of us that is fundamentally self-serving. If you're not careful, these ego-driven needs will lead you toward the traps of selfish, senseless, and spiritless giving.

No doubt you can conjure a mental image of someone being self-indulgent with their giving, like putting their name in huge letters on the building they endowed or paying all their family members questionably high salaries for sitting on the family foundation board. *I would never do that*, you might think, but self-indulgence is always easier to spot in others than in ourselves. This is one of the primary reasons so much philanthropy still goes off the rails at a time when the world has never been more in need of truly meaningful giving.

Before we go any further, let's delve into donor psychology and equip you with some tools for staying out of trouble. Giving differently and better means getting clear about how to find psychological fulfillment in healthy ways through your philanthropy. It also means avoiding the temptation of using your giving as a vehicle for ego-driven needs. This chapter will help you figure out your kryptonite, the self-centered need you are most likely to try to satisfy through your philanthropy. Now is the time to pay attention to this and take steps to meet those needs in a different way. Reflection and self-care illuminate the path of meaningful giving in a way that will make sense not only for you but for the world as well!

SEVEN UNIVERSAL HUMAN NEEDS

A great starting point for delving into your own psychology as a donor is the idea that we can understand human behavior on the basis of universal psychological needs. This goes back to Abraham Maslow and his hierarchy of needs. Maslow's hierarchy highlights what humans need for basic psychological wellness at its base and narrows as it explores what we need moving upward toward true psychological fulfillment. More recent contributors range from social psychologist Roy Baumeister to Tony Robbins and Chloe Madanes with their "Six Human Needs" framework. The model I find most powerful expands on Robbins's and Madanes's work and is built around *seven* innate human drives: security, novelty, social status, social connection, social contribution, self-evolution, and self-transcendence.

Even though all human beings share these same instinctive needs, the wide variety of human behavior we see around us every day stems from the equally wide variety of vehicles we choose to meet these common needs. This model is a great place to start if you are looking for some immediate, actionable insight into what makes you and those around you tick.

Innate Human Drives

We can think about these drives in two categories. First, there is a lower-level set of survival instincts or needs that we *must* find a way to meet in order to survive. These are basic, fundamental needs like food and shelter. The second category comprises a set of higher-level needs—we can think of these as a "calling" to live out our highest and best selves. Everyone is called to fulfill these higher-level needs for social contribution and self-actualization, but not everyone hears that call clearly or truly pursues it. Some of the greatest human pain and misery is caused when we never wake up and attune to our higher calling, or perhaps even more painful: when we hear the call clearly but fail to take the actions needed to respond and advance. I know from personal experience that it is no fun to hear a clear call to make the world a better place and not know how to answer that call with joy as well as impact. I lived twenty years of my life that way before finding a better path.

The Four Lower-Level Egocentric Needs

- **Security**: This need involves the basics, such as physical safety, shelter, and food. It also includes the need for a predictable, ordered environment.
- **Novelty**: Humans all crave some degree of entertainment, adventure, and surprise. If everything around us is entirely certain and predictable, we quickly become bored.
- **Social Status**: Everyone needs to feel like they matter to others and to themselves.
- **Social Connection**: At our most basic level, humans are social creatures. This means we are all wired to seek love. Some of us will end up settling for any form of connection with others, even when that connection is primarily negative.

The Three Higher-Level, Self-Actualizing Needs

- **Social Contribution**: Service to others can be a source of deep fulfillment and meaning, as well as a key that unlocks all the other needs. In other words, if you can find vehicles in your life for successfully contributing to others, you will meet all your other needs in the process.
- **Self-Evolution**: A sense of growth, progress, and personal development is vital to flourishing as a human

being. Unfortunately, not all of us figure out a way to meet this need. When we cannot satisfy our need to grow and evolve, we are blocked from a source of deep fulfillment.

- **Self-Transcendence**: The highest stage of personal actualization occurs when we become less focused on our sense of "self" and begin to appreciate how we are ultimately an integrated part of something much larger than ourselves. This perspective gives us the greatest leverage to see and transform the larger systems of which we are a part.

WHICH OF YOUR HUMAN NEEDS DO YOU USE YOUR GIVING TO FULFILL?

- Why does all this matter when it comes to you and your philanthropy? Remember, the very first commitment of meaningful giving is to *get visionary*. This is about conducting your giving in a way that prioritizes social impact above any of your egocentric needs. Let's be clear: you *need* to meet those lower-level psychological drives. We all have them, and we all need to satisfy them. The key is to find positive, creative ways of meeting those lower-level needs that don't get in the way of maximizing the impact of your giving.
- So, what's your kryptonite when it comes to bringing your lower-level needs into your giving? There are generally four problematic patterns to watch for.

Four Problematic Patterns

1. Giving to Gratify Your Need for Certainty and Security

There's nothing wrong with wanting clarity about the impact of your giving, and there is nothing wrong with wanting to protect and preserve valuable places and things. At the same time, it's important to consider how much you are leaning on your giving as a vehicle for creating security and certainty in your life overall. If you are, your giving may develop too narrow a focus. This prevents you from maximizing your impact on root causes and systems change. Systems change can be messier and more complex than simple forms of measurement and milestones allow. Likewise, preserving cherished places and things "above all else" can sometimes result in the unwitting preservation of problematic systems and structures beneath the surface. For example, there is a complex debate in New York City; Washington, DC; and other high-priced real estate markets about the extent to which historical preservation advocates and their donors have inadvertently impeded the supply of affordable housing. For better or for worse, the creation of local historic districts often results in restricting new construction.

2. Giving to Gratify Your Need for Novelty and Excitement

What if you hate to be *bored* by your philanthropy? That's not a problem in itself, but it is something to watch out for. Boredom can put us right at the slippery edge of using giving to gratify an ego-driven need for novelty. What might this look like in practice?

One form is going all-in on one new cause after another and moving on as soon as the next shiny object catches your eye. Boredom can also leave us more susceptible to growing enamored with dynamic, charismatic social entrepreneurs, throwing all manner of money and resources at them to back their visions, only to move on as soon as the next charismatic leader comes across our radar.

Giving to personalities who provide excitement or giving to causes that allow you to travel the world can be tempting on face value alone. When does this become self-indulgent? When it gets in the way of social impact. It could be totally compatible with social impact, but when your need for entertainment overshadows the actual benefit of your giving *for other people*, that's when you need to make a course correction. Are you giving to indulge a pet project that provides you some kind of excitement or entertainment value? This might look like buying a raffle ticket for a jet ski organized by an elite private school your own children attend. It might look like bidding in a silent auction for a travel adventure from an organization with an egregious track record. This is the case for organizations like the Disabled Police and Sheriffs Foundation, which was barred from soliciting contributions in 2019 after the Federal Trade Commission found it was giving less than 10 percent of what it raised to its supposed beneficiaries.[2]

3. Giving to Gratify Your Need for Social Status and Recognition

How important is it to you that other people know about your giving and that you receive recognition for doing it well?

Recognition could come in different forms:

- Immediate public praise and appreciation through various forms of publications, from e-newsletters to major media outlets
- Long-term elevation of your family legacy by naming buildings or other things likely to receive sustained public visibility
- Knowledge and appreciation of your giving by people whose social approval you desire, even if your giving is never widely publicized
- Knowledge and appreciation of your acumen as an impactful philanthropist by people whose professional respect you desire

There is nothing inherently wrong about any of these forms of recognition. However, they are slippery slopes. If you know recognition for your giving is a very important part of your own currency of fulfillment, it's worth exercising special care in order to avoid falling into the trap of selfish giving. Ask yourself, "Would I still make this gift even if I *knew* nobody else would ever know about it?" If the answer is no, that's a sign to look again and make sure this funding is also producing real, positive social impact that seems in some sense proportionate to the amount of money in question. If so, that's great! If not, then following through will take you into the realm of self-serving giving.

Remember, you always have another alternative. If there's something you absolutely, positively want to do for your own reasons, *you don't have to treat it as part of your philanthropy.* You can set your own standards for when you forgo tax deductions on expenditures that don't come with a reasonable level of social good. For example, I don't claim a charitable tax deduction for the gifts our family makes to our public school's PTA even though it's registered as a nonprofit. While its programs serve all children in the school, the benefits it provides are too focused on my own kids to justify this as an act of charity from my standpoint. I consider it more like a user fee for an after-school activity that I would appropriately pay for out of my own pocket.

4. Giving to Gratify Your Need for Social Connection

There's nothing wrong with using philanthropy to meet your needs for social connection. Indeed, when done with care, this can actually enhance the impact of your giving. However, if you find yourself leaning on your giving very heavily to meet this need, be careful. A donation to your grandchildren's already well-endowed private school or a donation to the large cultural institution of which your young adult child is a board member may help strengthen family ties, but is it serving a larger purpose? Is it in the public interest? You can also get into trouble when you become so personally close to longtime grantees that it becomes difficult to look objectively at the social impact of their work.

A great way to protect yourself from this particular kind of self-serving giving is to consider all the people involved. Ask yourself if your need to feel loved, cared for, or connected to any of these people might be overbalancing your focus on positive social impact. Likewise, consider whether there is anybody for whom you are so focused on expressing love and care that you might be losing sight of the social impact of your giving.

Clearly, it is important to learn how to recognize what spiritless, senseless, and selfish giving look like not only in others but for you *personally*. As you gear up your giving, it's crucial that you take steps to stay clear of these traps. Take the time to understand what each of these forms of giving looks like for you. In what ways are you most at risk of giving selfishly? In what ways have you given senselessly? What would a spiritless giving experience look like for you?

Most importantly, what would the most meaningful forms of giving look like for you? If you want to truly create meaning with your money, it's time to *get visionary*, *get real*, *get together*, and *get better*.

GETTING VISIONARY

The Ten W's for Donors:
Design Fundamentals for Your Giving

"[My] approach to philanthropy is not the only way.
It's just the one my resources and
opportunities inspired in me."

—MacKenzie Scott

Consciously or not, every donor comes to their giving with a unique combination of factors to incorporate and accommodate. Why not become more aware of and deliberate about the key considerations that shape the design of your giving? The better you understand what's driving your design choices, the greater your opportunity to land on meaningful giving that truly creates joy and impact.

When working with clients as they make plans to gear up their giving, I love to help people take themselves through a series of reflections. I've come to call these the Ten W's: worldview, wealth stance, wealth stock, why, what, which way, where, when, who, and whatever else. Identifying what's most important to you across this range of issues is a great way to elevate the impact of your giving out in the world. It's also a great way to maximize the sense of fulfillment and joy that your giving brings to you personally. And if you share authority over your giving with a spouse, other family members, or a business partner, walking through these design principles together is a great way to uncover areas of alignment as well as divergence—an essential step in taking your shared decision-making to the next level.

1. WORLDVIEW

It might not come to mind immediately, but one of the first things to explore is your own worldview. A worldview is a set of values and beliefs we use to make sense of the world around us. A person's worldview typically has both cultural and psychological components.

There are all kinds of ways to sort worldviews. I find one of the most useful approaches breaks them down into four basic categories:

- **Traditional:** Shaped by religious faith and cultural tradition

- **Modern:** Shaped by rational inquiry, the scientific method, and efficiency in economic production
- **Postmodern:** Shaped by a desire to address inequity, oppression, and inequality on a systemic basis, often grounded in a critique of traditional and modern social constructs for their role in perpetuating oppression and human suffering
- **Integral:** Shaped by a desire to embrace complexity and transcend polarization, integrates key elements of traditional, modern, and postmodern worldviews in pursuit of new approaches to addressing enduring social and political challenges

The Institute for Cultural Evolution offers an online assessment that will give you insight into which of these worldviews most closely resembles your own.[3] This is important because your view of how the world works has a significant impact on your approach to philanthropy. For example, what does it mean to *you* to make the world a better place? Articulating your worldview can be particularly helpful if you plan to work with others to carry out your philanthropy. The more others understand your philosophy of life and what you find meaningful, the better they can support you in finding impactful and fulfilling philanthropic opportunities.

Take, for example, the story of the Whitman Institute, founded in 1985 by Fred Whitman, an heir to the Crocker Bank fortune. As recounted by John Esterle, the Whitman Institute's longtime executive director, Whitman's passion was helping people make better-informed life decisions. His approach was grounded in experiences with mental illness within his own family as well as "a lifetime of instances where he felt irrationality and close-mindedness ruled the day." Esterle worked for almost twenty years as Whitman's trusted advisor, through many ups and downs. Whitman struggled to find projects that fully expressed his evolving perspective on life. His worldview was grounded in the rational, decision-making calculus celebrated by modernism. At the same time, Esterle recounts that Whitman had a yearning to stretch beyond these bounds. He wanted to engage complexity and innovate new solutions:

One reason he came to trust me, I think,
is because I never lost my sense of empathy for him
and his personal struggles, including his struggle
to find his own voice. He also knew that I genuinely
shared his passion for TWI's mission.

As he neared the end of his life, Fred Whitman decided to leave John Esterle in a position to take over full leadership of the Whitman Institute. After Whitman's death in 2004, Esterle took that opportunity to bring in new voices and partners. He went on to help found the Trust-Based Philanthropy Project. This peer-to-peer funder initiative has grown to over two hundred members, all committed to addressing the fundamental power imbalances between nonprofits and their donors. This is a mission that perhaps embodies the integral worldview Fred Whitman was feeling his way toward in his own lifetime.

2. WEALTH STANCE

One of the most fundamental questions to consider as you make plans to gear up your giving is how you relate to the resources you are giving away. How does your wealth inform your identity and your values? Are you the first in your family to create substantial wealth, or are you the custodian of a long-standing fortune passed down from one generation to the next? What is the ultimate purpose of your wealth? What goals will it help you accomplish? What is the portion of your resources that exceeds your needs? What are you prepared to give away, and on what basis do you determine that?

Not all these questions are straightforward, and getting to the heart of them can require some soul searching. A helpful way to undertake this inquiry is to consider three key dimensions of your relationship to wealth:

1. Your generational relationship to wealth
2. Your cultural relationship to wealth
3. Your goal orientation to wealth

As you explore this territory, psychologist Dr. James Grubman's book *Strangers In Paradise* provides a useful frame. He has worked with wealthy families over decades and developed the idea that adapting to affluence is akin to an immigration experience. This is a fitting metaphor. Contrary to popular understanding, 72 percent of the people who are currently among the ultra wealthy (above $30 million in investable assets) moved from working- or middle-class origins into this level of affluence in their own lifetimes. And only 7 percent of this group gained their wealth solely through inheriting it.[4] This means that most wealthy people are navigating a world they didn't grow up in, and even those who inherit wealth from their parents may still have a foot in each world. All of this can have significant implications for how you approach your giving, as Jennifer Risher details in her 2020 memoir *We Need to Talk*, a compelling first-person account of how her journey to wealth has played out in sometimes counterintuitive ways in the decades since she and her husband made their fortunes in the dot-com era.

Your Generational Relationship with Wealth

Are you a first-generation immigrant—what is sometimes called "G1" in philanthropic and wealth-advising circles? Are you G2, meaning that your parents made the transition into wealth? If so, you might have experienced this move to affluence during your childhood, in which case you have your own experience navigating this transition prior to becoming an adult. Or are you G3, the grandchild of the generation that first generated the family's wealth? If so, you have likely never experienced a different cultural and economic context.

Newcomers to the land of affluence find that it operates with very different norms and expectations than the working-class or middle-class cultures from which so many of the wealthy have come. As a result, each generation in this immigration journey faces a different set of challenges.

G1 has to adapt to a new set of cultural norms and expectations without a template from their own upbringing to guide them.

G2 has to navigate the pressures of coming of age within a unique cultural context that their own parents often do not fully appreciate.

G3 faces their own set of challenges relating to a world that views their privilege as native-born inhabitants of the land of wealth with distrust and resentment.

Your Cultural Relationship with Wealth

The immigration metaphor in Dr. Grubman's book points to three cultural stances around how you relate to your wealth: avoidance, assimilation, or integration.

Are you avoidant? This is the stance that people take when they want to maintain their connection to middle-class or working-class cultural origins at all costs. This leads you to avoid engaging with your wealth in many respects—for example, when you don't even tell your kids about the family's wealth out of fear that it will corrupt them and stunt their own sense of initiative and drive. This can create many unfortunate, unanticipated consequences for G2 and G3 because they end up not being prepared to navigate the world with a healthy relationship to their wealth.

Are you focused on assimilating into the world of wealth? This stance is about being richer than rich and completely leaving behind the trappings of the working-class or middle-class background from which you came. This, too, can be problematic because it doesn't lead to developing a healthy relationship with your wealth that is grounded in enduring values you can pass down across the generations.

Are you seeking balanced integration into the land of wealth? In this case you strive to retain the best of the middle-class or working-class values that lifted your family to affluence while also recognizing that there are valuable new ways of operating that allow you to make the most of your wealth while also serving a purpose larger than yourself.

Your Goal Orientation to Wealth

There are three key stages here:

1. **Aspire and Acquire**: In this mode, you are oriented toward growing your wealth. This doesn't have to mean that building a fortune is your primary motivation— it might simply be the consequence of other life aims, like building your own business or achieving success in some other field.

2. **Manage and Maintain**: In this mode, you are primarily seeking to successfully preserve and steward your family's resources once you have already reached a particular level of affluence.

3. **Distribute and Dispense**: You enter this mode when you come to feel that you have more wealth than you

need. Recognizing that "you can't take it with you," you become focused on making plans for sharing your wealth with others, whether within the family or through your giving.

It's possible to occupy multiple stages simultaneously. This is particularly likely if you are an active entrepreneur in a family with multigenerational wealth, which might require you to manage existing family assets and engage in estate planning as well as philanthropic giving while you are still actively growing a business. Indeed, lots of unanticipated complexity can arise as you navigate transitions in your cultural adaptation to wealth and your goal orientation, as entrepreneur and author Michael Sonnenfeldt chronicles in his book *Think BIGGER*. Drawing on his own experience resetting his relationship with wealth following the successful sale of his first business, Sonnenfeldt founded Tiger 21 as a peer-based support network for himself and other entrepreneurs who had successfully exited. It has since grown into a global peer-to-peer network for first-generation wealth creators, helping its members explore how money and meaning intersect across the different stages of their lives.

Now that you have some frameworks for considering your overall relationship with wealth, it's time to get even more concrete about how all this connects to your approach to giving.

Mapping Your Wealth and Your Giving Goals

A great way to get further insight on how your wealth stance informs your approach to giving is by charting out a lifeline for your net worth and your philanthropic giving. Begin by drawing a timeline that shows your financial net worth from your birth to the present. Then, extend this line all the way through to show the net worth you anticipate having at the end of your life. You can show the scale in dollar values if you want, but the real point is the shape of the curve. And yes, this does mean you are also reflecting on your expected life span. Next, chart out your annual philanthropic giving from your birth to the present. Project this line into the future to show the level of annual giving you anticipate through the end of your life. Go ahead and extend beyond your lifetime if you want to establish vehicles for giving that continue on.

When I am doing this exercise with clients, we lay these two charts side by side and consider how well they reconcile. Even if the scales are different, do the shapes of these curves correspond with each other? Are you okay with seeing your net worth diminish as your giving goes up? Do you want to reach the end of your life having maintained a certain level of wealth, or would you love to "bounce the check to the undertaker" as Chuck Feeney is on track to do? Feeney, the founder of Duty Free Shops, has given away the entirety of his $8 billion fortune during his own lifetime. Now in his nineties, he has reportedly reserved just $2 million to cover living expenses for himself and his wife.

While it might sound straightforward, this exercise can be surprisingly challenging to complete. Give it a try!

Your Philanthropic Posture

A second exercise for exploring how your wealth stance connects to your giving is to figure out your "philanthropic posture." This is about how you identify the resources you intend to give away. As the following graphic illustrates, there are several possibilities.

1. **Not currently giving significantly:** The first possibility here is that you're just not interested in philanthropic giving. Unfortunately, there are *lots* of people with the capacity to give who aren't inclined to do so. But we know you're not one of them since you're reading this book! The other possibility is that you are inclined to give, but your current income and/or wealth is below your own perceived threshold for having enough to be able to give in a significant way. This often happens when your goal orientation to wealth is still in an "aspire and acquire" mode. In this case, you might be telling yourself, "After I *make it*, I'll really get started with my giving."

2. **Giving from annual surplus:** You determine your level of giving each year based on your level of surplus from ongoing economic activity. This might be from employment earnings, investments, or profits from business ownership. Your net worth is probably growing or holding steady when you are in this position. This is where almost all of us start out in our giving. Some philanthropists continue operating this way even after the scale of their resources has increased by many orders of magnitude.

3. **Giving from clear corpus:** You have identified a chunk of your wealth that you know is surplus to your other needs, and you plan to give it away. You naturally get to this philanthropic posture when you have a "distribute

and dispense" orientation around at least some portion of your wealth. This doesn't necessarily mean you have the cash already on hand. You might also fit into this category if you are preparing for an anticipated wealth event, like the sale of a business, a stock offering, or an inheritance. Either way, you have decided to dedicate a defined body of wealth to your giving and are figuring out how best to go about it. Depending on whether you are still actively generating wealth, the relative size of your philanthropic corpus, and the pace of your annual giving, you may see your net worth decline over time as you give away these resources.

Where would you place yourself currently when it comes to your philanthropic posture? Again, there's no need to cast judgment on yourself—the point is simply to accurately assess your current approach. Then, ask yourself what it will take for you to feel ready to take the next step in your giving wherever you currently fall on this spectrum.

3. WEALTH STOCK

When you think about gearing up your giving, you might be primarily focused on the money you're planning to give away. However, money is far from the only form of capital you can give in a meaningful way. So, let's take an inventory of your wealth stock on a more holistic basis. Wealthworks, a project of the Aspen

Institute, has a helpful schema of eight forms of capital that go into building up the wealth of any given locality. This is a useful list when applied in the context of your philanthropy.

What is the stock of capital—in all these various forms—that you can draw on in pursuit of your philanthropic aims? On a scale of one to ten, how important is each of these types of capital to achieving the outcomes you are seeking in terms of impact and fulfillment? Likewise, on a scale of one to ten, how confident are you that your current stock of each form of capital is sufficient to take action effectively in pursuit of the outcomes you are seeking?

- Individual (time, physical health, autonomy to act, personal skills, and mindset)
  - Importance _____ Access _____
- Intellectual (ideas, knowledge, theory of change)
  - Importance _____ Access _____
- Social (relationships/connections/network, level of support from others)
  - Importance _____ Access _____
- Cultural (proximity, perspective, and shared systems of belief)
  - Importance _____ Access _____
- Natural (natural resources and other environmental assets)
  - Importance _____ Access _____
- Built (buildings and other physical infrastructure)
  - Importance _____ Access _____

- Political (alignment and level of support from key political actors)
  - Importance _____ Access _____
- Financial (money to make it all happen)
  - Importance _____ Access _____

Are there any important forms of capital to which you currently have insufficient access? What action is needed to bring a greater stock of these resources to take on the challenge? Are there some nonfinancial assets you have in abundance that you could leverage more powerfully in service of your philanthropic goals? For example, if you are a successful entrepreneur who has navigated the venture capital world and made a rewarding exit, you likely have all kinds of professional expertise (intellectual capital) and relationships (social capital) that could be profoundly valuable to well-matched social entrepreneurs looking to scale their ventures. Alternatively, perhaps you can leverage physical assets in creative ways. A great example of this is the Gates Family Foundation's renovation of the historic Hover building in downtown Denver. No, not *that* Gates Foundation—this Gates family built a business in manufacturing, not Microsoft. Through this single project, the foundation preserved a historic landmark, created a collaborative office space for many of its grantees, and housed the foundation's own operations, all in one beautifully renovated building. This is a great illustration of how thoughtful philanthropy can draw not just on financial capital but also on social, cultural, and built capital as well.

4. WHY

Why are you motivated to give? What will it actually take for you to feel joyful and fulfilled through your giving? The questions that follow are designed to help you achieve clarity about your own currency of fulfillment by reflecting on which of your core psychological needs your giving helps satisfy. Even though these questions don't begin with the word "why," they will help you get to the core reasons giving truly matters to you. It is important to answer these questions honestly and without judgment—there are no "wrong answers" here.

1. How important is it that I can measure the precise impact of my giving? How much certainty do I want to have that my dollars are being used in a specific way? How comfortable do I want to be that my giving will provide predictable, known value to others and to me?

2. How important is it that my giving serves to protect and preserve nonfinancial sources of value (e.g., religious traditions, works of art, physical places and spaces, cultural and civic institutions, etc.)?

3. How important is it that my giving provides a sense of adventure, exploration, and risk-taking?

4. How important is it that other people know about my giving and believe that I'm doing it well? How much does it matter that I receive recognition for my giving?

5. How important is it that my giving helps me feel loved, cared for, and connected to other people?

6. How important is it that my giving creates an opportunity for me to express love, care, and connection to others?

7. How important is it that my giving makes me feel like I am learning, stretching myself, and mastering new knowledge, skills, and mindsets?

8. How important is it that my giving creates a positive difference in the lives of specific other people—whether as individuals or collectively?

9. How important is it that my giving allows me to contribute to systems change and to making a lasting difference on the root causes of the problems I care most about?

10. If I had to choose a percentage of my giving that was focused only on addressing immediate needs and a percentage of my giving that was focused only on addressing long-term root causes, how would I ideally divide my giving between the two? Why is this my preferred ratio?

11. How important is it that my giving allows me to feel connected to something larger than myself and to deepen my understanding of what it means to be a human being?

12. Where am I on my own journey exploring race, identity, and power, and what, if anything, do I want my giving to help me learn about or act on in these areas?

5. WHAT

What do you really care about? As you gear up your giving, what meaningful impact are you seeking to make with your money? For some donors, these answers are already crystal clear, but for others of you reading this book, figuring out *what* to give to may feel like the most pressing part of your challenge.

If that's the case for you, here's some good news: it's an extraordinary gift to have philanthropic capacity that is not committed to a predetermined issue, organization, or cause. This gives you tremendous opportunity for meaningful giving because you can let your *why* help guide you to your *what*. This means you can solve for your joy at the same time as you solve for your impact. There are so many ways to create positive impact with your giving that you don't have to worry about giving up your own joy and fulfillment as a donor in the process. As we talked about in Chapter 2, your psychological needs are going to show up in your giving one way or another, so it's far better to solve explicitly for how your giving can help you meet your higher-level needs for personal growth, social contribution, and self-transcendence than to unconsciously use your giving to fulfill lower-level, ego-driven needs.

Whether you are starting from scratch or already have a chosen arena for your giving, the following questions can help you hone your philanthropic focus and maximize your impact on the issues that matter most to you. As a starting point, you probably already know that your own resources are limited when matched up against the scale of the change you hope to see in the world.

If you want to make a difference, how you focus your time and attention really matters!

1. What is your ultimate vision for a better world? What is true and flourishing in that world you hope to see, whether in your own lifetime or for future generations?

2. Many factors will likely have to come together to bring this ultimate vision for the world into reality. What particular element of this change story is calling most for *your* service? Is there a personal story or experience that leads you to focus on this arena of engagement?

3. What's the most audacious measure of impact in your chosen arena of engagement? What will be different when you and others have succeeded beyond your dreams within this arena and made the greatest possible contribution toward your ultimate vision of a better world?

4. What is the *one* thing that you *can* do such that by doing it, everything else on the path to achieving audacious impact becomes easier or even unnecessary? In other words, within your chosen arena of engagement, what is the most important contribution for you to make? In Gary Keller's book *The ONE Thing*, Keller underscores how vitally important it is to focus on the highest and best use of your time when seeking to achieve extraordinary results. In a similar vein, Jim Collins's book *Good to Great* introduced the idea of the "hedgehog concept"

as a way to figure out exactly how to focus a business for unique success in a competitive market. Here's an adaptation of this idea for forward-thinking philanthropists. Your *one thing* is at the intersection of these four spheres:

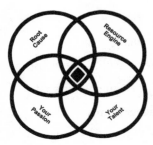

● Root Cause — What's causing the problem in your Arena of Engagement?
● Resource Engine — What can reliably provide money and other assets (not just your own!) to solve the problem?
● Your Passion — What do you love doing?
● Your Talent — What are you great at doing?

5. What are the lagging indicators of your successful impact as a donor? When you achieve success pursuing your one thing, how will you know?

6. What are the daily, weekly, and monthly activities that constitute leading indicators of your philanthropic impact? In other words, what is the mission-maximizing output (MMO) for your giving?

7. What can take place without you? Take a step back and imagine that you had to take yourself completely out of this whole situation. What if this change-making effort had to be carried out while you were completely side-lined and couldn't lift a finger to help? Think witness protection program or an alien abduction. Whose ideas would be needed to move forward? Who would need

to take action on those ideas? What institutions and which individuals would need to connect and work in concert?

8. Now, bring yourself back into the story. Is there anything you want to add, emphasize, or amend about your philanthropic focus and how you carry out your giving moving forward?

MacKenzie Scott's approach to giving is a good illustration of how you can take yourself out of the story while still focusing your giving toward producing a transformative impact on the issues that matter to you. By working with a team of philanthropic advisors, she has found leaders and organizations who are already leading the way in the fields she wants to focus on, such as higher education, opportunities for women and girls, and combating economic and racial inequality. She has simply backed them with no strings attached. In the first two years of her giving program, MacKenzie Scott has given away over $12 billion without getting any fancier than this.

Even if you don't feel clear yet about the issues that matter most to you in your giving, don't let that stop you from getting started. Sometimes one of the best ways to discover your what is simply to learn by doing. Stay tuned for more on how to apply the principles of a lean startup to get going with your "minimally viable philanthropy" in the next chapter.

6. WHICH WAY

It's important to determine which style of giving is best for you when it comes to translating your resources into truly meaningful giving. Figuring this out starts with taking a closer look at four functional roles in any change-making ecosystem: stakeholder, entrepreneur, accelerator, and advisor. Which of these are the best fit for you as you carry out your giving?

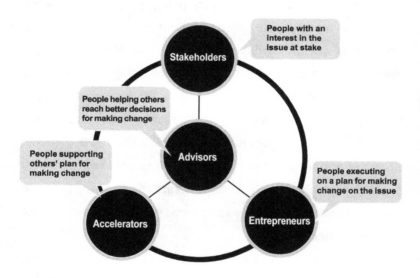

Entrepreneurial: In this style of giving, you and your immediate team are the ones generating the ideas as well as the operational strategy for making change. Your path to impact and fulfillment is about mobilizing and engaging others around an effective plan. Then, you work that plan and give it everything you've got. This is the kind of strategic philanthropy practiced by donors who not only develop their own "theory of change" but who go on to issue RFPs and other casting calls to enlist grantees as players in their strategic plans. The entrepreneurial style also fits those who pursue their vision for social change by directing their active business operations toward a social purpose. Take, for example, Australian mining entrepreneur Andrew Forrest. He is putting his $8 billion fortune into play with dramatically outsize investments in R&D that bet his company's future on clean-hydrogen technology and carbon-neutral production of iron ore and steel.

Accelerative: In this style of giving, your path to impact and fulfillment is about being a talent spotter. You find great leaders and organizations with great ideas for making change on the issues that matter most. Then, you do everything you can to speed them on their way. There is plenty of scope for being strategic in this role, but you operate more at the big-picture level and not so much at the operational and programmatic level.

Advisory: In this style of giving, you are focused on helping others generate the best possible ideas and decisions on their own terms. You draw on your expertise, access, and knowhow to do so. This is not typically your primary giving style if you define yourself as a "donor," but it may still be a vitally important part of how you operate and add value to others. An advisory style of giving may be especially important for you if your "wealth stock" includes a lot of intellectual, social, cultural, or political capital. There's a parallel here with the role that angel investors play in financial markets—adding value to the early-stage companies they back not simply with their financial investment but also by leveraging their own business experience, networks, and other forms of capital to help these startup ventures succeed.

Stakeholding: In this style of giving, your own experience and proximity to the issue is a source of inspiration and ideas for addressing it. Some of the most effective entrepreneurial givers are also stakeholders with proximity to the issue they are working on. For example, Dustin Moskowitz and Cari Tuna focus on reshaping the culture of philanthropy by helping fellow donors give more effectively. They do this through their support of all kinds of infrastructure for the effective altruism movement through Open Philanthropy and other projects. Another example is philanthropist and author Lisa Greer, whose book *Philanthropy Revolution* uniquely leverages her insight as the recipient of many fundraising asks to help nonprofits connect more effectively with donors. On the flip side, entrepreneurial donors who drive hard on a strategy without having a stakeholder's proximity to the issue at hand face a significant risk of misfires and blunted impact.

Remember, these giving styles are not mutually exclusive. Within any given issue area, it may be possible to show up as an advisor, as an entrepreneur driving a plan, and as an accelerator of the efforts of others. Similarly, on the issues that matter most to you, perhaps you are already a stakeholder with an interest in the outcome no matter what other roles you play.

To get to the heart of which way of giving makes the most sense for you, ask yourself two questions. First, if you could only play one of these roles as you move forward with your philanthropy, which would it be? And second, which of these giving styles matters the *least* to your sense of impact and fulfillment? This self-reflection and honesty is a key consideration as you gear up your giving.

7. WHERE

The question of geographic focus is fundamental to many people's philanthropy. Perhaps you already know for sure that you want to focus your giving in a specific place, like your home town or state, for example. Perhaps you're considering an even tighter footprint, like the Harlem Children's Zone, with its laser focus on just ninety-seven blocks in New York City. Even if the issues you are attracted to are global in nature, it's rare that your giving will unfold without any geographic considerations whatsoever. The following questions will help you gain insight into how geography intersects with your philanthropy.

1. Does a Certain Place Play a Primary Role in Your Giving?

Do you have a clear geographic lens for your giving? At the tightest level of focus, this might be a specific property, such as a wilderness preserve or a particular neighborhood. Other defining geographies might be your home city or state or somewhere overseas to which you have a strong connection. If you do have this kind of defining geographic commitment in your giving, here are some important questions to consider:

- What makes this place so meaningful to you?

- If you were barred from giving away any of your resources to this place or area, what would you do instead?

2. Do Some Places Play a Role in Your Giving for Secondary Reasons?

Even if you don't have an immediate geographic preference, does the *what* and the *why* of your giving have geographic implications nevertheless? To revisit our example of Dustin Moskovitz and Cari Tuna, their commitment to effective altruism is grounded in the idea that people have equal intrinsic value regardless of their circumstances. At first blush, it might seem like this *what and why* is explicitly global in its scope. However, in practical terms, their giving philosophy leads this couple to focus on specific places with outsize opportunities to relieve human suffering at scale, such as by addressing neglected tropical diseases in places like sub-Saharan Africa and Southeast Asia.[5]

With this in mind, are there any second-order considerations that inspire you to focus your giving in specific places? Are you led to these geographies simply as a logical conclusion in order to maximize the impact of your giving? Are there any other ways that focusing on these places contributes to your sense of fulfillment as a donor?

3. Who Has Proximity to the Places Where Your Giving Is Focused?

When it comes to giving that makes sense, proximity matters. This is especially true when addressing complex challenges where solutions are emergent rather than preestablished. Being close to the action as it unfolds allows you to spot patterns and new possibilities. How much time do you physically spend in the places where your giving is focused? Would spending more time there yourself lead to greater impact or personal fulfillment? Is that even an option for you? Are there others in your world whose proximity to these places you can constructively draw on? One easy way to do a proximity audit on your giving is to look through your cell phone contacts and email address list. How many people do you see there with a presence in the places where your giving is focused? What roles do these people play in the decisions you make about how you do your giving in that place? Are these contacts stakeholders, entrepreneurs, accelerators, or advisors?

No matter where you land after your proximity audit, stay tuned. There's more on how you include others in your decision-making under the ninth W (Who), and in Chapters 9 and 10.

8. WHEN

There are three key questions to work through here:

1. When Do You Plan to Get Started?

Perhaps the answer to the first question is already obvious to you. "I'm looking to gear up my giving now! That's why I'm reading this book." That's great, but actually following through on your intentions is trickier than it seems. There are many well-intentioned would-be philanthropists whose money is still sitting on the sidelines years after they told themselves it was time to gear up. Don't fall into that trap of senseless giving! Audit your intentions on timing:

- Is there an external force requiring that you act within a certain time frame?
- Is it totally up to you when you take action on your giving?
- How consistently have you acted on your philanthropic intentions so far?

If you suspect that you might end up procrastinating, what can you do to strengthen your propensity to act? Consider what already works for you in other areas of your life when you want to follow through on your intentions. We will discuss this in detail later in Chapter 12.

2. When Do You Plan to Fully Exhaust Your Resources and Conclude Your Giving?

What is your time horizon for spending your philanthropic resources?

- Right away, ASAP: I want to go for broke and spend down as fast as I can
- Within a defined period of years that is shorter than my own anticipated lifetime
- Within my lifetime
- Within a defined period following the end of my life

- Perpetuity: I plan to establish an ongoing philanthropic vehicle
- A hybrid option (e.g., a certain amount in the next ten years; an additional amount by the end of my lifetime; the rest spent in perpetuity through an ongoing philanthropic institution)

Remember the lifeline exercise from earlier in this chapter where you mapped out your net worth and your annual giving? Here's a chance to redraw the curve on your annual giving to best reflect your latest thinking on how much giving you want to do from year to year moving forward. Let's look at some of the factors you might consider in determining which of these options truly makes the most sense for your giving.

- Tax and financial planning considerations regarding the timing of your giving
  - Have you already established philanthropic vehicles that have specific, time-bound distribution requirements or opportunities?
  - Are there any hard parameters that arise from your choice of giving vehicles, estate planning, or other tax and financial planning decisions you have already made?
- Nature of the issue you are seeking to address
  - Does the challenge you are focused on have a meaningful deadline? An example of this would be helping more athletes from developing nations compete in the next Special Olympics.

- Is there a possibility of a breakthrough solution in your arena of engagement such that the need for further investment would diminish or go away entirely? An example of this would be research to cure a disease or advocacy to enact a sweeping policy change. In this case, you might want to push hard for that breakthrough as fast as possible.
- Is the need in your arena of engagement evergreen? An example of this would be educating successive generations of children within a particular cultural tradition. In this case, you might want to parcel out your resources steadily over time or even in perpetuity.
- Is your philanthropy aimed at reducing immediate suffering on an urgent basis, like providing relief aid for victims of a natural disaster? If so, you'll have a clear and compelling rationale that drives the timing of your giving in response.

- Family dynamics/intergenerational issues
  - How important is it to have philanthropy be a point of connection between successive generations of your family?
  - How will you approach trade-offs between inclusion and alignment when it comes to having family members involved in grantmaking decisions?
  - How will you approach trade-offs between maintaining family control of governance and having board members with expertise and proximity on philanthropic priorities?

3. When Do You Plan to Fit Your Philanthropy into Your Schedule of Existing Time Commitments?

It's crucial to consider how much of your own time you are prepared to spend on philanthropy. Certain kinds of giving, such as systemically oriented, strategic philanthropy are more time intensive than others, but there's no fixed amount of time you have to spend to give meaningfully. The answer is going to be specific to you and your circumstances. Everything is valid, from a full-time, forty-plus-hours-per-week pursuit to setting aside just an hour or two every few months, or even making a one-time decision to completely vest your philanthropic resources with someone else. It can be helpful to actually draw this out by adding another lifeline to the chart referenced in this chapter. This new line will show how much time you plan to spend on your giving moving forward. When you compare the shape of this line with the timeline for your annual giving intentions, you'll gain insight into how much—if any—help you need from other people along the way.

9. WHO

Who is involved in carrying out your giving? Decision-making friction is one of the biggest drags on donors looking to gear up their giving. All things being equal, the more people you share authority with, the more energy it takes to make decisions. But going it alone has major drawbacks too. First, you may not have time to make all the decisions needed to keep things running smoothly. Second, you may not have the passion, proximity, or expertise to make the best possible decisions on any number of issues. This is why it's so important to carefully consider who else should be involved and what roles others will play in the decision-making process.

Sharing Authority with Family Members and Close Associates

Let's start with family members, business partners, and other close associates. Consider a simple example involving just one other person with whom you make decisions. This might be a spouse, but it could also be a sibling, son, daughter, or business partner—anyone with whom you share philanthropic resources and accountability. The following graphic outlines three different scenarios for how your philanthropic interests and decision-making authority intersect.

Separate Interests & Spheres of Authority — You — Your Partner

Intersecting Interests & Spheres of Authority — You — Your Partner

Fully Overlapping Interests & Spheres of Authority — You & Your Partner

If you already share authority over your giving with a family member or business partner, which of these scenarios comes closest to your reality? How comfortable does your current arrangement feel? Does it work equally well for each of you? Would some other approach to sharing authority bring more joy and/or more impact to your giving?

After over a decade of advising philanthropists, I have found that fully shared decision-making authority between spouses or other close relations is the most difficult scenario to pull off. It's rare for two people's philanthropic interests to coincide completely, so there's often an appeal in having at least some separation between spheres of authority—you do your thing, and I'll do mine.

In addition, making all decisions jointly can take a lot of time and energy. Doing it well requires a willingness to explain your thoughts and feelings to someone else. There's both an upside and a downside here. Sharing decision-making authority has the potential to improve the quality of your giving. For example, it could make you less likely to be selfish in your giving because you'd be embarrassed to have self-serving motives subject to scrutiny by someone who knows you well. But to the extent that having to explain yourself causes you to hang back from making decisions, it also elevates the risk for senseless giving, where you and your partner end up giving with less joy and less impact together than you would if you divided your resources and made decisions on your own.

The takeaway is simply this: the greater the divergence between you and your partner's answers to the questions in this chapter, particularly your *what* (philanthropic focus) and your *why* (psychological motivation), the more work it will take to make decisions jointly. Determine how committed you are to communicating with each other across differences, and proceed accordingly. There's no right or wrong answer here. If you want or need to share decision-making authority over your giving with a spouse, sibling, parent, or business partner, the most important thing is that the two of you have clarity about your arrangement and a commitment to operate in a way that works for each of you—and for everyone else out there counting on you to make the most of your giving.

Do You Need to Bring on Staff and Advisors?

If making decisions jointly with those to whom you are closest is one potential barrier to gearing up giving, another is getting the kind of outside help that truly makes sense for you and the issues you care about. Adding advisors or other staff to your philanthropic decision-making is a big step. While it may solve and streamline some processes, it also introduces principal-agent dynamics that ultimately make your giving process more complex. So, let's be sure that adding staff or advisors makes sense for you before you go down this road.

Six Options for DIY Giving

Below is a series of options for how you could proceed with little to no help from paid staff or advisors. As you go through this list, take note of how you react to each. Are any of these off the table for sure—if so, why? Do any of these options seem like appealing paths forward? Could some combination of these approaches be a good fit?

1. **Go Simple and Straightforward**: Pick a simple issue with a clear, causal chain and only one or a very few potential grantees to choose from. For example, it's easy to support the local soup kitchen and have confidence that your money is doing real good for real people, even if it's not necessarily addressing the root causes of food insecurity in the community.

2. **Go Blue Chip**: Pick one or more name-brand organizations that have a reputation for leading the field on the issues you care most about, and back them in a substantial way. Take, for example, Nike founder Phil Knight's 2016 donation of $400 million to his alma mater, Stanford University.

3. **Go Boutique**: Commit whatever time it takes upfront to diligently seek out a handful of organizations whose leadership you can get to know and trust and whose strategy you believe in. Then, back them for the long haul. A great example of this approach comes from Don and Doris Fisher, founders of the Gap. They went looking for innovative public education ideas to support back in the mid-1990s. They eventually identified two fledgling organizations: the KIPP network of charter schools and Teach for America. The Fishers went on to support these organizations with decades of donations totaling hundreds of millions of dollars.

4. **Go Passive**: Pick a mutual fund rather than individual stocks. This is what you are doing when you entrust

your philanthropic resources to the United Way or a more specialized, pooled fund. You are allowing others to allocate funding on your behalf, and ideally they have both passion and proximity when it comes to the issues you care about. One of the best-known examples of this approach is Warren Buffett's decision to vest almost all his philanthropic resources with the Bill and Melinda Gates Foundation. After doing this, he held a seat on the foundation's board for a time. Recently, he has stepped back from even that level of involvement, content to let others make the grant-making decisions. If you take this approach, consider choosing a vehicle whose decision-makers are themselves members of the community to which they are directing funds, such as the Southern Power Fund or Black Voices for Black Justice Fund.

5. **Go With Your Gut**: This is about following your interests and instincts when it comes to your giving. Let the chips fall where they may; shoot from the hip; see what sticks—pick your metaphor, but they all amount to going with your gut. If you already have well-honed instincts based on your proximity to and passion for the issues you care about, gearing up your giving doesn't actually have to take that much time. An extreme example of this might be Frances and Patrick Connolly, the couple from Northern Ireland who gave away more than half their £114 million in

lottery winnings within a year. They did this by simply writing down a list of people and organizations they wanted to support. As one of them said, "We didn't set out to give half away; that's just what happened. We sat down and looked at the list and kind of figured out what we thought would make a difference in people's lives."

6. **Go Pro**: Commit a substantial amount of your time and essentially become your own professional advisor/staff. Develop trusted relationships with key leaders on the front lines of the issues you're focused on, and build your strategy in tandem with them. Do your own diligence on prospective grantees, and get close enough to the work to track impact and make course corrections as your giving unfolds. Some of the largest-scale practitioners of this approach prefer to operate below the radar. In my time as an advisor, I have come across several donors who are quietly giving away tens of millions of dollars every year with no staff whatsoever.

So, what do you think? Is it viable for you to proceed without bringing on your own staff or advisors as you gear up your giving? Again, there are no wrong answers. The key to figuring out the best strategy for maximizing your impact and joy starts with being honest with yourself.

Mapping Your Philanthropic Decision-Making Process

One really useful way to get a handle on all the issues related to who is involved in your giving is to map out your decision-making process. Whatever role others play in your giving right now, chances are this will evolve over time. The following chart shows a key set of decision-making areas across the top row and a range of people who might be involved in these decisions. The chart is filled in using the following codes for the role that a given person plays in a particular decision-making arena:

Propose: The person is responsible for bringing forward a proposed course of action.

Decide: This person makes decisions.

- D=formal authority as ultimate decision-maker
- d=one vote among a larger group, majority rules
- *D*=informal authority as ultimate decision-maker (whatever the rules formally say)

Consult: This person is asked for input about a decision before it is made.

Inform: This person is told about a decision once it is made.

Execute: This person is responsible for carrying out the decision once it is made.

Person	Overall Strategic Decisions (e.g. vision, mission, plan for achieving social impact)	Governance Decisions (e.g. legal structure, membership of governing body/ies, hiring of executive leadership)	Decisions on Allocating Funds for Social Impact	Decisions on Allocating Funds for Financial Return	Management Decisions (e.g. hiring & management of nonexecutive personnel, oversight of accounting and finances, operational policies and procedures)
You					
Spouse/Partner					
Children					
Grandchildren					
Parents					
Brothers/Sisters					
Cousins					
Other extended family					
Friends/associates					
Friends/associates of other family members					
Paid staff					
Paid consultants					
Unrelated volunteers					
Third-party legal fiduciaries					
Your grantees					

The idea with this chart is to fill it in twice. First, map out who is involved in your giving right now and at what level of authority. Next, map out your current best thinking on your ideal decision-making structure in the future. Who is involved in your giving, and who is doing what after you get geared up?

If these two charts are significantly different, it's possible you may have some mixed feelings about moving forward. For example, if you are starting out as a "checkbook" philanthropist, the first chart you fill in will be pretty simple. You will have a whole lot of decision-making authority, and there won't be too many other names on the board. This is one reason making the transition from doing things on your own can feel so challenging. You know that your own time is limited. By adding others into the process, even if it's just your spouse, let alone staff and advisors, you are introducing more decision-making friction points. You are also exponentially increasing the need for communication. Who really matters! A lot of people with significant philanthropic capacity get stuck on the trade-off between the streamlined decision-making of a DIY approach and the enhanced capacity and potential impact of a staffed approach. If this sounds like you, chances are you'll want to dig more deeply into this. When we get to Chapters 9 and 10, we'll walk through options for staffing up and working effectively with others across all the dimensions of your giving.

10. WHATEVER ELSE

Before you go any further, now is the time to identify whatever else is important in your giving. It can be helpful to think in terms of "hard parameters" (e.g., legal and regulatory requirements for which absolute compliance is required) and "soft parameters" (e.g., personal preferences like family considerations that are subjective in nature but often no less important to those involved!). Here are some questions designed to help you identify your own hard and soft parameters. As you go through these questions, be sure to ask yourself, "And what else matters here?" There are almost always specific factors that are unique to each individual looking to gear up their giving.

- At this point in the chapter, can you think of any strongly held beliefs that haven't come up yet? Now is the time to identify any key beliefs that are likely to shape your outlook on your giving.

- Are there any particularly pivotal experiences that have shaped your perspective on giving? Is there an example of a peer or mentor you feel inspired to follow?

- Are there any specific tax and/or financial-planning considerations that will influence your approach to your giving?

- Are there any relevant family dynamics or relationships that haven't already come up in response to previous question prompts?

- Are there nonfinancial resources you'll be drawing on to carry out your giving? This is where it can be helpful to reflect on your own stocks of capital—the eight forms of wealth we looked at earlier. Are there any particular considerations that arise for you around your own individual capital, such as your physical health and well-being? What about your intellectual capital, such as the ideas and knowledge you can use to inform your giving? And what about social capital, cultural capital, natural resources, physical infrastructure, and political capital? Are there any particular opportunities and constraints that arise for you and your philanthropic approach in these domains?

Overall, what else matters to you in your approach to giving? Only you can fill in these blanks. Now is a great time to identify whatever else might influence how you move forward.

PUTTING IT ALL TOGETHER

At this stage, you are already well on your way to gearing up your giving. So much philanthropy goes on without careful consideration of the factors you just reviewed, often with unsatisfactory results. Push yourself to synthesize the Ten W's outlined in this chapter. Come up with a design thesis *in the form of a question* that incorporates the most salient design features you have surfaced throughout this chapter.

Here's a sample design thesis for a couple in their late forties. Their goal is to spend down their philanthropic assets within their own lifetimes. They have decided not to involve their children, and they are using a private foundation alongside a donor-advised fund in which they have already vested their philanthropic assets.

How might we double the volume of our giving to $6 million per year, moving beyond the large institutions we know and are personally involved with in our home community? And how could we do so spending no more than one hour per week on our giving while still having confidence that we are creating substantial positive impact advancing racial equity and economic opportunity in a neighboring state where our family has its roots?

Pulling everything together in this form is helpful because of how it encapsulates your key design considerations while also giving you permission to continue ideating and experimenting as you move forward. You don't have to answer this design question all at once, but the clearer you are about what is most important for creating joy and impact with your giving, the more likely you are to succeed.

GETTING STARTED

Strategic Philanthropy Is Not the Only Way

> *"Start where you are. Use what you have. Do what you can."*
>
> —ARTHUR ASHE

Warren Buffett, who pledged to give all his wealth away in 2006, has to date only managed to put 50 percent of his Berkshire Hathaway shares into the Gates Foundation. In the meantime, his overall net worth has doubled. At over ninety years old, he is only one-third of the way toward his goal of giving away his wealth during his own lifetime.[6]

How many years have you known that you had significant resources to commit to philanthropy? Perhaps more specifically, how long have you been *intending* to gear up your giving without actually taking action? It's no secret among philanthropy advisors that people who have built up the wealth to be philanthropic in a major way sometimes struggle to actually get started. At first glance, this appears counterintuitive; these are people with genuine intentions to make the world a better place. However, all too often these same individuals get stuck thinking that the *only* responsible way to maximize the impact of their giving is to do something they don't really find fun or fulfilling: engage in the arduous and intense process of "strategic philanthropy." As a result, these donors put off their giving and don't act on their very real, very genuine intentions to be more philanthropic. More often than not, these philanthropists fall into the trap of senseless giving.

The Bill and Melinda Gates Foundation, with its professional staff numbering in the hundreds, has pursued strategic philanthropy in the US education space for years. One example is its Measures of Effective Teaching project. This took place over three years and involved multimillion-dollar grants to six school districts chosen through a competitive selection process. The project drew on 3,000 volunteer teachers and produced 20,000 hours of videotaped lessons. A bevy of researchers hired by the foundation then analyzed these recordings to identify which instructional practices were most highly correlated with student gains on academic assessments. This perfectly worthy endeavor resulted in valuable findings for the field, but such an intensive, donor-driven philanthropic strategy is not a fulfilling, attractive approach for many donors no matter how significant their philanthropic capacity.

Whether or not the term "strategic philanthropy" means anything to you, let me ask you this: when you think about gearing up your giving, whose ideas are you planning to back? Yours or someone else's? Strategic philanthropy is most appropriate when you have your own theory of change and your own ideas about how best to make change and you are determined to invest your resources accordingly. Here's how Paul Brest, the godfather of strategic philanthropy, puts it:

> The term 'strategic philanthropy' [is] synonymous with outcome-oriented, result-oriented, and effective philanthropy. This is philanthropy where:
>
> - donors articulate and seek to achieve clearly defined goals;
> - they and/or their grantees explore and then pursue evidence-based strategies for achieving those goals; and
> - both parties monitor progress toward outcomes and assess success in achieving them in order to make appropriate course corrections...
> - ...The case for strategic philanthropy ultimately is based on the belief that the intentional, systematic, and rational pursuit of an outcome increases the chances of achieving it.[7]

Who wouldn't want to associate themselves with these worthy goals? This is the rational, modernist worldview in all its glory: rigorous, evidence-based philanthropy as the true path to maximizing social impact. In the most extreme version of this approach, your grantees function like contractors hired to carry out particular pieces of your strategy to your precise specifications.

Strategic philanthropy has been so celebrated by some of the largest donors and leading lights in the field that it would be all too easy to conclude it is the only option that makes sense for thoughtful, caring philanthropists. Strategic philanthropy can indeed be a meaningful way to achieve impact if you are ready and willing to follow through on all of its demands (including true partnership with those closest to the ground), but it is *not* the only way to create both impact and a deep sense of fulfillment with your giving.

Four Functional Roles in Advancing Social Change— Which Ones Are Right for You?

Recall Chapter 3's discussion of the four functionally defined roles when it comes to advancing social change. Whatever issue you are focused on, it's important to understand which roles you play within the change-agent ecosystem. Often, this means stepping back from the common labels of "funder" and "grantee."

Stakeholders: This is often the broadest category, including any and all people with an interest in the issue in question. For example, everyone living in the Colorado River watershed is a stakeholder when it comes to water conservation and allocation policies.

Entrepreneurs: These are people with an idea *and* an operational plan for making change on the issue in question. Entrepreneurs may be first movers, but they also typically seek to organize and enlist others in pursuit of impact. Take, for example, the work of climate activist Greta Thunberg, known for organizing a youth-led movement of school strikes and other direct actions to protest inaction on climate change.

Accelerators: These are people who use their resources (financial and otherwise) to get behind someone else's plan for making change on a given issue. MacKenzie Scott's philanthropy ($5.7 billion in 2020 to three hundred or so nonprofits working across several distinct issue areas) is a classic example.

Advisors: These are people who use their knowledge—and perhaps also their social, political, and cultural capital—to help others make better decisions in pursuit of making a positive impact. In some cases people carry out this role as their professional focus, like the teams at Building Impact and other philanthropic advising firms do. In other cases, nonprofit leaders do double duty as informal advisors to philanthropic institutions. Similarly, some experienced foundation executives and individual donors spend much of their time advising fellow donors as well as social entrepreneurs.

These roles are not mutually exclusive. You might wear several different hats within the same social-change ecosystem. It's particularly important to recognize that if and when you decide to pursue strategic philanthropy, you are very often assuming the role of entrepreneur in the social-change ecosystem. This means you are the one developing the plan, and you are the one most likely to seek out and enlist others. If you want to play the role of entrepreneur on a complex social challenge, you need to stay close to the stakeholder communities and deeply understand the dynamic nature of the work. This is true even if you consider yourself a "funder" or a "grantmaker" as the Gates Foundation and other practitioners of strategic philanthropy typically do.

The Paradox of Strategic Philanthropy: Money on the Sidelines

Paradoxically, the heavy emphasis on strategic philanthropy across the field is leading to billions of dollars sitting on the sidelines. It has resulted in lots of giving gone wrong.

Strategic philanthropy is really hard to do well; it demands a lot of the donor. In fact, strategic philanthropy may well be the riskiest option because it takes a lot of knowledge, skills, mindset, and resources to pull off.

What are the key prerequisites?

- **Knowledge**: The more complex the dynamics surrounding the issue you want to focus on, the more important practical proximity is to figuring out the path forward.
- **Skills**: You or people on your team will need to be able to think critically, evaluate evidence objectively, and formulate your strategy accordingly.
- **Mindset**: A rational, modernist worldview is often helpful here. You will also need a fair amount of patience.
- **Resources**: You will also need time, human capital, and financial capital.

Further, strategic philanthropy is even harder to get right when the problems you are interested in are complex and the solution cannot be fully engineered in advance. This is where it's helpful to make the distinction between three types of challenges: simple, complicated, and complex.[8] When the problem is simple, the answer is almost always straightforward and reliable. If you do A, then you can count on B as a result every time. Solving a simple problem is like following a recipe: you can reliably produce a desired result by carefully following the instructions the same way each time. Similarly, complicated problems also have solutions that are linear causal chains. However, they have many more steps, and each one represents a potential critical failure point. If the causal chain breaks at any point, you won't receive the result you are going for. This is what NASA must grapple with when launching astronauts to the space station. The name of the game here is to engineer as much risk out of the situation as you can through careful cross-checks and quality-control procedures.

Complex problems, on the other hand, are a different kind of challenge entirely. The solutions to complex challenges are emergent. They are properties of dynamic, adaptive systems, so you can't follow a linear chain of cause and effect to reliably arrive at the same result every time. A classic example is the difference between raising your first child and your second child. They are different people influenced by an array of different circumstances too complex to control. If you want to tackle complex challenges, you will need even more knowledge, skills, and resources, as well as a patient and resilient mindset.

Finally, as a field, philanthropy's overemphasis on strategic philanthropy as the gold standard too often results in donors winding up with spiritless, senseless, or selfish giving.

When donors feel trapped in the straitjacket of their own

strategy, their philanthropy can feel spiritless. They end up planning, evaluating, and course correcting their giving with an ever-diminishing sense of happiness and fulfillment. When strategic philanthropy becomes a joyless endeavor, giving begins to feel like a mechanical duty. When philanthropy feels like a chore, it is often because the philanthropist has become weighed down with metrics, milestones, and other reporting requirements, all of which disconnect them from the meaning of their philanthropic work.

Strategic philanthropy can transform into senseless giving because strategic philanthropy not only is unappealing to many donors, but those who *do* get involved can become afraid that doing anything else would be irresponsible and lacking in rigor. They end up diminishing or delaying their giving as a result. For too many donors, gearing up to really get their giving "right" becomes something like a time-intensive home renovation project that keeps getting put off for "someday."

Finally, selfish giving arises when donors pursuing strategic philanthropy don't have the level of maturity and humility to reckon with the reality of the world as it actually is. As a result, they end up building a fantasy world with their philanthropy, which does damage to all concerned.

Six Alternatives to Strategic Philanthropy

The good news is strategic philanthropy is *not* the only way to maximize your impact, and it sure isn't the only way to find personal fulfillment and joy in your giving. Here's an outline of six options to consider:

1. Seed and Speed

This is angel investing and human capital building for individual, early-stage social entrepreneurs. The "seed" part of the equation is that you provide early-stage resources for social entrepreneurs who are just getting started. Being one of the first donors to back a new leader and a new idea means you will always know your resources made a genuine difference. Sure, there is risk here because many new ventures may not succeed immediately (or ever), but that comes with the territory. You can take measures to increase the "hit rate" of your early-stage investments through upfront diligence if you choose. And bear in mind that you might not need to do as much formal diligence as you think if you are backing leaders with proximity and passion and you are willing to view learning itself as a positive return.

The "speed" part comes with supporting human capital development in various forms for these leaders and backing them as full human beings. This might involve supporting their participation in incubator and accelerator programs or supporting them in receiving coaching, mentorship, and so on. There are all kinds of challenges that early-stage entrepreneurs must confront and overcome. Helping them grow personally and professionally is not only a great way to boost their success; it can also feel deeply fulfilling for you as a donor. This can be particularly true when you have the opportunity to hear from your grantees about what a profound difference this kind of support makes. *And almost nobody in the donor community supports the "speed" part of this equation by backing their grantees at the intersection of personal and professional growth.* So you'll have no doubt about attributing the impact of whatever resources you commit toward accelerating the personal and professional growth of your grantees.

2. Equip for the Trip

This is what you might call *expeditionary giving.* You are providing significant backing for a social entrepreneur to go on a voyage of discovery, exploring new territory. This is a great approach when the challenge you are interested in is complex and nobody—even those with expertise, passion, and proximity—can map out the path to success in advance. In these situations, the way forward has to be discovered as it emerges. You might say this is a form of strategic philanthropy, but the point here is that you are *not* positioning yourself as the entrepreneur responsible for developing a strategy (nor are you simply hiring someone else to carry it out). Instead, when you "equip for the trip," you are backing a promising social entrepreneur as they embark on their own voyage of discovery, now in partnership with you. Your responsibility is to equip the expedition the best you can initially and then to be a reliable partner as the journey unfolds (entrust, discuss, adjust). Yes, this means you have put your faith in someone else's vision and strategic instincts, but you can also use this approach to lean into the advisor role. In this position, you can operate as a true sounding board and strategic partner, helping map out course corrections if needed and providing flexibility in resources to pursue emergent paths as the front-line entrepreneur encounters challenges. A great example of this is how the Emil Schwarzhaupt

Foundation provided ongoing, flexible general operating support and a strategic sounding board during the Civil Rights Movement. When the emergent strategy of movement-building organizations and leaders became clear, the foundation was ready to follow through with further support.

3. Wings Without Strings

The idea here is to put wind beneath the wings of well-positioned change agents. This comes in the form of completely unrestricted general operating support, letting the agents of change soar entirely on their own terms. This is what MacKenzie Scott has been making headlines for. In 2020, she kicked off her philanthropic efforts by giving away $5.7 billion to US-based organizations with strong track records of past success and/or significant potential. This spanned several areas of interest to her, including social services, racial equity, economic development, and environmental protection. Her team of advisors lightly vets these organizations through desk research and one or two phone calls, and then she funnels a bunch of cash in the form of a one-time grant of general operating support. Often, this is the largest single gift these organizations have ever received, and it arrives in their bank accounts with no application process, no strings attached, and almost no subsequent reporting requirements. In its most expansive form, this approach would be like the MacArthur prize on steroids, giving unrestricted support to change agents with proximity and passion. Offering "wings without strings" honors the power of people on the front lines to address the challenges that matter most to our shared future and allows them to have at it in whatever way they see fit.

How does this differ from "strategic philanthropy?" For one thing, this approach doesn't involve ongoing evaluation and oversight of grantees and their operations. This is not to say that the donor can't engage strategically at a macro level to assess how the effort is going over time. MacKenzie Scott shows us how you can move extremely large amounts of money without creating a large, standing philanthropic infrastructure. You can do this by working with a consulting team, streamlining your vetting process, and attaching few, if any, ongoing reporting requirements for grantees. With this approach, you simply identify the organizations you want to support and write very large checks, no strings attached. No intricate strategy is needed beyond identifying the general areas and types of leaders you want to support.

4. Maintain and Sustain

The idea here is to provide ongoing support for established entrepreneurs who are creating ongoing value within an established footprint. These leaders and their organizations might have been expeditionary at one point, but now they are all about maintaining a steady state of service within existing boundaries. You can experience tremendous joy and impact as a donor by backing these folks on an ongoing basis. It doesn't need to be new or scaling toward some larger vision to be worth supporting year in and year out. Too many donors have dismissed this kind of giving as lacking excitement, but it can actually be incredibly meaningful and impactful to have a long-term supportive partnership with an organization that is living out its mission of service day to day within a defined boundary. Take, for example, the Harlem Children's Zone, which has focused on breaking the cycle of intergenerational poverty within a defined ninety-seven-block neighborhood of New York City for decades. Many of its donors, including Board Chair Stanley Druckenmiller, have been steadfast supporters of this journey going back fifteen years or more.

5. Outsource without Remorse

This is about placing your philanthropic resources in the hands of a dedicated team with proximity and passion and letting them allocate your resources for maximum impact. This team can use the principles of strategic philanthropy so you don't have to, developing a theory of change and an evaluation function and making ongoing adjustments to grantmaking strategy based on evidence of impact over time. They could also operate using the other approaches, such as Seed and Speed and Equip for the Trip. There's an exciting opportunity here to create space for those closest to the challenges you care about to make allocation decisions that are grounded in the wisdom of their own proximity and lived experience. The key to recognizing whether this is the right approach for you as a donor is whether you can wrap your head around finding true fulfillment for yourself at this level of distance. Will it feel psychologically satisfying enough to receive periodic progress updates from your delegated team *without* being involved in the day-to-day decision-making and operations? For some donors, the answer is an emphatic yes! No remorse here and no fear of missing out.

6. One and Done

The idea here is to make a single, big gift that transfers your philanthropic resources in one fell swoop. There are all kinds of options for doing this. It could be there is a particular institution whose work you find so inspiring that you simply want to entrust your entire philanthropic capacity to them. Another alternative is an extreme variant of Outsource without Remorse, whereby you transfer your entire philanthropic corpus to an intermediary, which then makes grants according to its own logic with no ongoing involvement or influence on your part. Warren Buffett has landed on this approach by announcing his intention to vest his entire philanthropic capacity with the Bill and Melinda Gates Foundation and subsequently stepping down from their board. You could place certain restrictions on your gift, or you could give the recipients carte blanche to do with it whatever they will.

This approach might be appealing if you don't have the need or capacity to be involved in an ongoing way and you have a clear interest in a particular cause, institution, or organization that is already doing work in the field. Some might criticize this approach as too risky and unstrategic—after all, you are placing your entire philanthropic legacy in the hands of others and hoping for the best. However, placing your trust in those who are closer to the action to make more effective decisions than you *can be a deeply disciplined and strategic choice*. And there's no question that the opposite is far worse. Holding onto your philanthropic resources without giving them away is the most senseless and unstrategic path of all.

Find What Works with Minimally Viable Philanthropy

Maybe you feel immediately drawn to one of these alternative approaches to strategic philanthropy. Maybe you are sure you want to reject certain others out of hand. Or maybe strategic philanthropy, with all its rigors, really is best for you to maximize both impact and personal fulfillment in your giving. One of the best ways to figure out what kind of giving really makes the most sense for you is to give yourself permission to proceed with what we call "minimally viable philanthropy." Anyone who has spent time in the startup world will recognize this term. In the lexicon of lean startups, the MVP acronym refers to a minimally viable product. The idea is that when you are in startup mode, you want to get something out in the marketplace generating consumer feedback as soon as you possibly can—even if that product is far from perfect and even if it falls embarrassingly short of what you ultimately envision. Until you test your ideas in the real world with real consumers, you don't know if you're building dream castles in the sky or if you're actually on the path to creating something that meets a real demand in the marketplace.

A simple shift in thinking can be really valuable in translating this lean startup approach to your philanthropic giving. Instead of "I need to figure this out before I really gear up my giving," try this on: "I need to gear up my giving before I really figure this out." An

MVP approach is a great way to see if your vision shows real-world promise. It is also a good way to determine if it will offer you the kind of personal fulfillment you find meaningful. In fact, there are all kinds of benefits from learning as you go, and this experience can prevent you from making irrevocable decisions about your legal and tax structure, staffing, focus, key grantees, and more.

Here are some tips on how to successfully proceed with your MVP:

- Work with a consultant to simulate your preferred staffing structure if you're not ready to commit to permanent hires. Hesitancy around building a team and having to spend time finding the right people, managing them, and so on, is one of the biggest stumbling blocks for people looking to gear up their giving. It might seem self-serving to say this, as our firm has been providing consulting services in this very space for over ten years, but the reality is that in most cases, securing the help of a dedicated consultant is a smart investment. It makes a lot of sense to spend a comparatively small amount of money early on with someone who's had dozens of experiences building the kind of thing that you are building for the first time. Would you build an addition to your home without hiring an architect? Only if you were deeply committed to a DIY approach! After all, you don't have to hire someone who's going to move into that home with you. And even though some of the most effective partnerships with trusted advisors can feel almost like family, you don't have to set the bar at this level just to get started.

- When you are hiring consultants, look for those who have spent a lifetime answering a calling to make the world a better place. This is why social entrepreneurs often make great trusted advisors for your philanthropy. Chances are they have a deep, intrinsic motivation that will prompt them to do the right thing. *This includes the vitally important responsibility of getting real and telling you things you don't want to hear.* It could be that you're already working with a pro bono trusted advisor on your giving and you don't even know it. Is there an outstanding nonprofit leader in your field of interest who you find yourself calling when things get sticky? I know from spending a lot of time working with dynamic social entrepreneurs in our accelerator program that they are fielding these kinds of calls all the time!

- Pilot on a small scale. Create some form of constraint, whether geographic or time based. Then give yourself permission to iterate multiple times within those constraints. The Harlem Children's Zone began as a one-block pilot program in the 1990s, evolving and growing over time to serve ninety-seven blocks. Along the way, this became a nationally known model for a place-based, anti-poverty investment strategy.

- Proceed prior to trust. This might sound like an irresponsible thing to do, but the reality is that one of the most powerful ways to build trust is by placing your trust in others before you know them deeply. You aren't actually risking as much as you might think. What is the worst that could happen if this person or this organization doesn't turn out to have the capability or integrity that you hoped for? It's quite likely that the more significant risk is holding back in your giving. When you're standing on the sidelines, you have no chance at all of achieving a positive impact with your resources. Additionally, social entrepreneurs with a genuine calling to their work have an amazing well of integrity and intrinsic motivation to do their very best. They really are working to make their corner of the world a better place. You can actually trust the great majority of them, sight unseen, to show up with integrity in pursuit of impact. The chances of getting outright defrauded by established social entrepreneurs are quite low. If you are starting small, there's often no better way to assess capability and competence than to see someone in action.

- Define a window for testing, evaluating, and course correcting. Give yourself permission to change course as a result of what you learn. A great example of this is how the Lynch Foundation addressed the challenge of helping to train school leaders in the Greater Boston area. Beginning in 2010, it supported an initial cohort of just twenty aspiring leaders to participate in a fourteen-month fellowship. Each year since, the Lynch Leadership

Academy at Boston College has refined its program on an iterative basis. It has since served over two hundred fifty school leaders statewide, including more than half the actively serving principals in the city of Boston. Peter Lynch, who made his fame and fortune picking stocks for Fidelity's Magellan Fund, explains how a willingness to take risks and learn from mistakes translated into the Lynch Foundation's giving strategy: "I think in philanthropy, becoming more effective is trial and error. You try approaches, you try methods, you keep refining it, and you learn from mistakes."[9]

- Don't neglect to communicate with other stakeholders. They need to know what you are doing is preliminary and subject to change. Establishing this helps ensure you can preserve flexibility and be responsible in setting expectations.

Make a Move

One of the mantras of a lean startup is "fail fast." It's worth considering what "failure" even means as you gear up your giving. It's not a failure if some people question your choices. If you place your trust in someone you later discover lacks the knowledge, skills, mindset, luck, or resources to produce the impact you hoped for, you still have not failed. The real failure is *inaction* or allowing hesitation and distrust to pull you into senseless giving. Whether you want to commit to full-bore strategic philanthropy or whether you want to pursue one of these six alternative approaches, a great first step is to commence with minimally viable philanthropy. Don't be afraid to learn by doing. Get your resources onto the field and into the hands of those with the proximity and passion to make lasting progress on the issues that matter most.

GOING BIG AND MAKING IT COUNT

Five Ways to Achieve Transformational Impact

"Imagination encircles the world."

—ALBERT EINSTEIN

Sometimes donors get stuck because the impact they believe they can have with their giving doesn't feel big enough. A concern I hear a lot goes something like this:

Our family doesn't have tens of billions of dollars
like the biggest foundations and philanthropists.
We want to know that our dollars are actually making
a difference in the world. We want to feel like our giving

really matters. How do we make an impact we can
hang our hats on, one that makes us feel like
we're making a genuine difference?

No matter which particular issues you focus on, there's value in "thinking big" with your giving. This is about going for transformational change with whatever level of resources you're bringing to the table.

1. TRANSCEND HYPER-PARTISANSHIP AND POLARIZATION

In the United States—and in many countries across the world—we have never been more divided. What if we could advance the work of social change without having to beat our opponents in a political death match? What if you could use your giving as medicine for what divides us? In his 2018 book *Decolonizing Wealth*, author and activist Edgar Villanueva describes the power of philanthropy when it successfully harnesses money and redeploys it to heal and unite people.

Done well, your giving can frame issues in ways that build a larger constituency around lasting solutions. In fact, there's a promising school of thought and practice emerging along these lines. For example, as the political philosopher Steve McIntosh wrote in his 2020 book, *Developmental Politics*, "The good news is that the daunting problem of our dysfunctional democracy is creating the developmental pressure we need to 'think anew and act anew,' as Lincoln famously said. Although further regression is certainly a real possibility, the fractured state of American society also has the potential to catalyze a cultural renewal that can lead to a new era of political cooperation and progress."

Steve McIntosh isn't alone. In 2021, author and award-winning journalist Amanda Ripley explored how even the thorniest conflicts can be resolved in her *New York Times* bestseller *High Conflict*. That same year, performance and leadership specialist Jamie Wheal published *Recapture the Rapture*, a bestseller that investigates the power of intentionally constructed communities to transcend conflict from a position of neuroanthropology.

Transcending partisanship and polarization starts with appreciating how different worldviews have led us to focus on what divides us rather than what unites us. An elevated perspective can find points of commonality even in seemingly bitter conflicts. The core practice is to celebrate what is most valuable for each side's perspective. Then comes integrating these best attributes into something new that transcends the conflict.

The marriage equality movement is an excellent example of how this has worked in real time. In only twenty years, support for marriage equality in the United States went from 20 percent to almost 80 percent. The Supreme Court then made it the law of the land.

How was this massive, sweeping change accomplished? Advocates framed the issue of marriage equality in ways that integrated key values from all three major worldviews. Values of love and family spoke to those with a traditional worldview. Values of caring and fairness spoke to those with a postmodern worldview. And values of individual freedom spoke to those with a modern worldview. In the end, this reframing and demonstration of value became an unstoppable message capable of reaching the hearts and minds of the American public.

Leading philanthropists are increasingly incorporating this focus on transcending partisanship and polarization into their giving. For example, Laurene Powell Jobs and the Emerson Collective sponsored the fellowship that allowed Amanda Ripley to do the deep research behind her groundbreaking book on conflict resolution. And the Einhorn Collaborative's work establishing the New Pluralists project is an emerging example of how philanthropic institutions and individuals can come together across differences to focus on bridging what divides us. Launched in 2021 during the height of the pandemic, Einhorn has helped convene a dozen donors from diverse perspectives into a funders' collaborative that collectively supports over forty organizations working to embrace differences and solve problems together across the civic spectrum. These issues range from racial reconciliation to immigrant inclusion and interfaith engagement.

2. EXPLORE THE UNKNOWN AND EXPAND THE BASE OF HUMAN KNOWLEDGE

Discoveries, once made, permanently expand the stock of human knowledge. Philanthropy that supports the creation of knowledge has an opportunity for tremendous leverage. Some of the clearest examples involve medical research on curable diseases. Consider the crowdsourced "ice bucket challenge" of 2014. In only six weeks, this internet craze managed to raise $115 million to support ALS research. Those resources funded two breakthrough discoveries on previously unknown sources of the disease.[10] Another example is how the Gates Foundation's support helped the scientific community develop a vaccine against malaria. It has been a long road: Gates first announced $168 million to support this effort in 2008. A dozen years and a billion dollars later, the world now has a vaccine with clinically proven efficacy in preventing childhood malaria.[11]

If you are going to fund research, here are a few ideas for getting even more bang for your buck:

- Find overlooked areas. Take global security and conflict resolution. Less than 1 percent of philanthropy goes to this arena, creating the potential for outsize impact. Consider the Hewlett Foundation's $500,000 grant in 1984 to help found the Harvard Negotiation Program. This program and its faculty have since pioneered many advances in the art and science of negotiation and conflict resolution. Along the way, they have trained thousands of practitioners and helped resolve conflicts in some of the world's most troubled regions.
- If you have an appetite for playing the odds, focus your research funding on "black swan" events. These are

situations where the chance of a breakthrough discovery is small but the payoff is huge. An example of this might be funding research to identify meteors that are on a potential collision course with Earth.

- When it comes to understanding the impact of the research you support, don't insist on sole attribution. Be okay with knowing that you were one of many who made a contribution to a breakthrough. Many of the most consequential discoveries are bigger than any one donor or single research team.

- Take an expeditionary approach with your research partners. You are making a voyage of co-discovery that requires patience and trust. Sometimes research is like a phase transition. Much energy and effort has to be put in before the water boils—before there is a breakthrough.

3. ENGAGE IN ADVOCACY (AND POLITICS) TO INFLUENCE THE FLOW OF PUBLIC SECTOR RESOURCES

Many issues that matter a great deal take massive amounts of resources to address. Public education and affordable housing are two examples. One of the most leveraged ways for philanthropists to engage on these issues is by influencing how public dollars are allocated.

There are several key pathways here. One is to influence policymakers' choices through lobbying and other forms of advocacy. Another is to influence who is actually in office by engaging in electoral politics. Yet another is to work on reforming the rules of our electoral system itself. As Katharine Gehl and Michael Porter point out in their book *The Politics Industry*, breaking partisan gridlock and special interest power is one of the most leveraged ways to support policymaking that better aligns with the public interest.

And yet, too many donors hang back from advocacy and electoral engagement. So let's address four of the concerns we most often hear from these donors.

- **"It's against the rules to support lobbying and advocacy with my charitable giving."** Not true. Most nonprofit organizations are permitted to lobby, and almost every type of vehicle for charitable giving is allowed to provide support to these entities. Even private foundations can make gifts to public charities that engage in advocacy and lobbying. To do so, they must restrict their funds to non-lobbying activities, and the gift can't exceed the total amount the organization spends on non-lobbying activities. Under certain circumstances, it's even possible for a private foundation to make grants to noncharitable advocacy organizations, commonly known as 501(c)(4)s. The Alliance for Justice has published a set of very helpful guides on this topic. There are some details that need close attention here, but the general point holds. You can gain lots of leverage from supporting lobbying and other forms of advocacy. With care, you can do so within the bounds of the applicable rules and regulations.

- **"Political giving is not tax deductible."** True, but so what? You can engage in political giving as an individual with personal funds. You can also donate through an LLC, which is one reason more and more high-capacity donors are using them. So, think twice before you put your entire philanthropic corpus in a vehicle that can only make charitable gifts. By doing so, you are giving up a key source of leverage.

- **"Political giving feels dirty and broken."** It may feel dirty, but it's definitely not broken. Political giving actually works very well to influence public policy and public spending. That's why those looking to advance their own interests at the expense of the public do so much of it. Don't leave the field to be dominated by those who are in it for selfish reasons.

- **"We're stuck. Our democratic system is hopelessly gridlocked and there's no way to change it."** This is exactly why it's so important to consider the ultimate-leverage play when it comes to political philanthropy: investing in changing the rules of our democracy to better serve the public interest. It won't be easy to institute rank-choice voting and revamp the procedural rules of

Congress, but it isn't necessarily a pipe dream if enough people are willing to come together around these aims. These reforms would do much to transcend the extreme polarization and gridlock that interferes with scaling viable, valuable solutions to all kinds of issues.

4. LEVERAGE AND CHANNEL THE POWER OF MARKETS

Why not harness the power of markets as part of your change-making strategy? Far too often donors approach their giving purely as charitable grantmaking. For example, let's say you have a private foundation, and you distribute the required 5 percent of the corpus each year as grants to charitable entities. What about the other 95 percent? It doesn't have to just sit there in traditional investments. Think about how much more leverage you can get from investing those charitable assets in ways that are aligned with your values and your change-making goals. These days, many donors are finding that mission-aligned investing is not concessionary. What this means is you don't give up a market rate of return to align your charitable asset investment strategy with your vision for a better world.

There are several ways to do this:

- Place an ESG screen on your investments. In other words, invest only in companies that meet certain environmental, social, and governance standards. An increasing array of money managers and investment banks now offer these funds. Recent research by investment bank Morgan Stanley found that ESG-screened investment funds performed on par with the market going back more than a decade. What's more, these funds have also enjoyed lower downside risk because of a reduced likelihood of corporate scandals.[12] As promising as ESG investments can be, it's still wise to do your due diligence in selecting them to avoid the risk of "greenwashing," a term used when ESG claims are not backed up with real evidence.

- Make program-related investments (PRIs). In this way, you can put your foundation's assets to work in alignment with your vision for change. PRIs typically involve accepting low or no return on a financial basis, but their social impact can be transformative. Rather than making an outright grant, a PRI might take the form of a revolving loan fund in which you make capital available to mission-aligned organizations at low or no interest. Because of their concessionary nature, they can also be counted toward your foundation's 5 percent annual giving requirement.

- If you are operating an active business, consider how you operate your business as part of your change-making strategy. Take Australian entrepreneur Andrew Forrest, who has pivoted his mining company into a clean energy infrastructure, making massively outsize investments in R&D to develop clean hydrogen technology.

Then there are people like Tony Davis, someone who brings all three of these market-harnessing strategies together. After a successful stint as a co-founder of the Anchorage Capital Group, he stepped aside from the hedge fund world and set up his family office. From the start, he maintained a philosophy that there was no reason to separate his efforts to make the world a better place from his ongoing engagement in the market as an investor. He set up his family office to deploy his assets for making change across the full spectrum, from charitable grants all the way to maximizing market investments. His vision for social change ultimately led him back into the market to help others do the same. He founded the Inherent Group as an SEC-registered investment fund focused on sustainable ESG investments, not just for his own money but for others as well. It operates alongside the Inherent Foundation, through which he continues to engage in charitable grantmaking and PRIs.

5. DON'T JUST WORK IN THE FIELD OF SOCIAL CHANGE—WORK ON THE FIELD OF SOCIAL CHANGE

One of the greatest points of leverage you can have in your giving is to positively influence the people around you. You want to encourage and support others who are engaged in the field, whether they are fellow donors, social entrepreneurs, leaders, or community members. Getting behind others' proximity and passion for the issues that matter most is one of the most meaningful things you can do with your money.

Here are four ways to make the most of this opportunity:

1. Engage Your Fellow Philanthropists as a Generous Presence and a Trusted Advisor

This is all about showing up for others to help them have more impact and experience greater personal fulfillment from their giving. You can help them get more out of their giving journey by asking two questions. First, what would make for extraordinary impact and fulfillment in their giving? And second, what is the single biggest challenge standing in their way? After they respond, simply look around your world for ways you can help.

Very often, our first instinct as enthusiastic donors is to enlist others in our own ideas for giving. But some of the most effective and influential philanthropists take a stance of *radical hospitality* with their peers, creating welcoming spaces for learning and development across a broad range of philanthropic aims. Take, for example, Laura Arrillaga-Andreesen, the founding donor of Stanford University's Center on Philanthropy and Civil Society. Founded in 2006, the center brings together students, researchers, and practitioners to pursue three goals. Their website lists them as follows:

1. *Expand the body and reach of quality research on philanthropy, civil society, and social innovation.*
2. *Increase the pipeline of scholars, practitioners, and leaders in philanthropy and civil society.*
3. *Improve the practice and effectiveness of philanthropy and social innovation.*[13]

MONEY WITH MEANING

Stanford PACS has gone on to publish the *Stanford Social Innovation Review*. This journal is a leader in its field and shares a wide range of best practice ideas in the arena of social change and philanthropy. The center also offers a variety of sought-after training programs and materials aimed specifically at philanthropists and their staff members. As Stanford PACS has grown and evolved, it has attracted many other donors to serve on its advisory board.

2. Invest in the Full Humanity of Social Entrepreneurs

One of the most leveraged ways to feel outsize impact is to get behind early and midstage social entrepreneurs. Support their impact *and* their personal growth and joy. Think of this as "guardian angel" investing. Social entrepreneurs feel their calling so strongly that they are often leading from a personally sacrificial place. Those patterns of leadership often lead to burnout and blunt their long-term impact. So, make a rule that when you get behind a social entrepreneur's venture, you also get behind their personal wellness and flourishing. You won't find many other donors focusing so directly on the personal and professional growth of these leaders and their teams. Your involvement here means you will know that your giving is playing a unique role in this venture's continued success and social impact.

This is also a rare instance when I'm telling you *not* to provide general operating support. You will likely need to specifically earmark some resources to support wellness and personal growth.

Otherwise, many social entrepreneurs are going to tell you they want every single dollar to go to their organization. This doesn't mean you should force them to enroll in a specific program or self-care regimen. What it does mean is that you should tell them you have another pot of money they can draw down when they come back to you with a specific idea for their personal growth. Another barrier these passionate leaders are likely to have is a desire to take care of their teams before themselves. That's a fine impulse on their part, so consider making a similar offer to support their team's growth and development on the condition that they have first presented a plan for drawing down the funding to invest in themselves. This is exactly what the Margulf Foundation has done with their program of Health, Wellness, and Sustainability grants. They offer these to every single organization in their portfolio. This program represents a rare instance in which they restrict the money given to grantees—these funds can *only* be spent on wellness and self-care. What's more, the organizational leadership has to spend at least some of it on themselves before they can spend it on their teams.

If you want to take this strategy to the next level, get behind programs that are delivering support to whole cohorts of social entrepreneurs. For example, the Pahara Institute was one of the early leaders in this arena among education-focused social entrepreneurs. There is also a group of outstanding cohort-based programs supporting leaders of color, such as the Surge Institute and Camelback Ventures.

3. Democratize High-Impact Social Change: Billions by Millions

Inspiring others to give and helping fund the infrastructure that enables them to do so can be a deeply satisfying and impactful way to gear up your own giving. This is about supporting the agency of people closest to the challenges so they can generate and resource their own solutions. This includes everything from supporting community-organizing initiatives to participatory grantmaking. It also includes supporting the infrastructure for community-based giving initiatives. A great example of the latter is 4.0 School's Angel Syndicate. This initiative brings Black community leaders together to activate themselves as philanthropic change agents.

4. Full-Scale Wealth Transfer to Visionary Social Entrepreneurs: Billions to Brilliance

What if one or more signatories to the Giving Pledge created ten $1 billion LLCs and handed control of these vehicles to ten MacArthur-style geniuses with proximity and dedication to addressing the needs of their communities? This goes beyond grant support. This is about literally transferring wealth to visionary social entrepreneurs on a truly significant scale.

The simplest way to do this would be to pay the taxes on the amount transferred. Those selected would end up with something like 60–80 percent of the original capital. The rest would go to the public sector in the form of taxes. Recipients would then be entirely free to deploy these resources as they saw fit. It would truly be their money. Does this sound crazy? What's far crazier is that the vast majority of signatories to the Giving Pledge have seen their wealth *continue to accumulate* despite their intentions to give at least half of it away in their own lifetimes.

Even if you don't have billions to give away, consider what your version of this strategy might look like. What's your vision of the MacArthur prize on steroids? Which incredibly gifted change agents with proximity, passion, proof, and promise can you get behind in a radically big way? How much joy and impact could you set free in the world by taking this leap and putting your money behind the transformative genius of others?

It's easy to get the impression that donors looking to gear up their giving need to set up a big, strategic apparatus to invest their philanthropic resources effectively. Thankfully, this just isn't true. You can go lean and find both impact and fulfillment with your giving.

GETTING ORGANIZED

Structuring Your Giving for Maximum Impact and Joy

"Form follows function."

—Louis Sullivan

Let's assume at this point you've got some form of minimally viable philanthropy going. Now, the key question is: what legal and organizational structures are best suited for meaningful giving?

To be clear, what follows is general and *not* legal advice, nor can it account for all of your particular circumstances. Everyone's situation is different. Statutes and IRS regulations are subject to change, sometimes on short notice. For all these reasons, you should thoroughly consult with your legal counsel and other professionals as you make decisions around structuring your own giving.

FORM FOLLOWS FUNCTION

Remember the Ten W's? The *what, when, where,* and *who* of your giving are all important design considerations when it comes to structuring your approach from a legal and organizational standpoint. It also makes sense to consider two more of the Ten W's as you get real about what legal and organizational structures will serve you best. Which forms of *wealth stock* are you planning to deploy in your giving? And don't forget to take a look at *whatever else* is important to you, particularly from a tax and financial planning perspective.

Let's start by reviewing the most common structures through which you can carry out your giving. We'll then go on to look at key functional questions that will help inform your choices.

SEVEN STRUCTURAL FORMS FOR YOUR GIVING

Broadly speaking, there are seven main options to consider as you decide how best to structure your giving. Donor control is far from the only factor you'll want to consider, but it is often top of mind for those who are planning to expand their giving. So, for the sake of clarity, we'll go through these, moving from those that offer more control to those that offer less control, whatever their other benefits.

1. **Checkbook Philanthropy:** You make charitable gifts as direct personal expenditures. This is the natural starting point for many of us, simply supporting the

organizations and causes we choose by making direct contributions from our personal funds. In fact, even for people whose resources have increased dramatically since they began giving, checkbook philanthropy is often still the default setting.

2. **LLC:** You create an entity in the form of a limited liability corporation (LLC), and it carries out your giving program as well as any other business activities you assign to it. This is a relatively recent innovation when it comes to structuring philanthropy. It is increasingly utilized by a number of high-profile, ultra-high-capacity donors, such as Priscilla Chan and Mark Zuckerberg. This approach doesn't offer a charitable deduction upfront, but when the LLC makes charitable contributions, those tax deductions pass on to the LLC's owners. The biggest attractions of this approach are the tremendous flexibility and privacy that it offers, as well as providing a layer of liability protection for the LLC's owners.

3. **Private Nonoperating Foundation:** You create an entity that qualifies for federal tax exemption under section 501(c)(3) but is classified as a private foundation. You vest resources into that entity and make grants to recipients you select. This is a traditional path commonly known as a "family foundation." It offers full control over the foundation, as well as the opportunity for the foundation to continue operations under the leadership of successive generations of family members. Of

course, in practice, a number of high-profile foundations established decades ago by founders like Henry Ford and Andrew Carnegie no longer have any family-member involvement. Why doesn't everyone just set up a private foundation and be done with it? There are limitations for private foundations, such as lower tax-deductibility limits on contributions and more restrictions on assets they can receive. Private nonoperating foundations also generally have greater liability and an increased administrative burden.

4. **Private Operating Foundation**: You create a private foundation that uses substantially all of its assets to carry out direct service programs instead of grantmaking. This allows you to apply to the IRS for recognition as a private operating foundation. The primary advantage of this status is that donations to an operating foundation are eligible for deduction in the same manner as donations to public charities. Otherwise, operating foundations are generally treated in the same manner as nonoperating foundations. This option is typically used by donors who wish to be social entrepreneurs themselves, as it enables them to carry out specific programs to address issues directly.

5. **Supporting Organization**: You create an entity that functions in close partnership with an existing public charity, typically a community foundation. This allows you to carry out your giving program under the auspices

of a public charity. This approach is not widely used because of the administrative and regulatory complexity involved in establishing and maintaining a supporting organization. It also gives the founder less control than they would have with a private foundation. Still, some high-capacity donors have utilized this approach to benefit from the increased charitable deduction rate for gifts to public charities as opposed to private foundations. Donors also have the opportunity to be more closely involved in the operations, investment choices, and governance of the supporting organization than is possible through, say, a donor-advised fund (which is the other option for conducting your giving through a public charity).

6. **Donor-Advised Fund**: You make an irrevocable gift of resources to a public charity that assumes full ownership and legal responsibility for these assets. Donor-advised funds are becoming increasingly popular vehicles for giving. Fidelity and Vanguard Charitable are two of the larger players in this space, but most community foundations also offer them to donors. The funds are maintained in a segregated account and disbursed to grant recipients at your recommendation. This approach provides administrative simplicity but less flexibility and control.

7. **Philanthropic Fund**: You transfer resources to an intermediary that aggregates funding from multiple donors

and carries out its own giving program. The United Way is perhaps the most widely known example of this approach. A number of community foundations also operate in this space, offering "field of interest" funds to donors. In recent years, a whole new generation of pooled philanthropic funds has arisen, such as Blue Meridian, Co-Impact, and the Freedom Fund. These funds offer donors a way to address issues for which solutions at scale require more resources than a single donor can provide on their own. They may also create opportunities to connect with and learn from those who have greater proximity to and understanding of the complexity surrounding key issues. Another important variety of philanthropic funds is purpose-built public charities, such as New Venture Fund, which serve as fiscal sponsors for carrying out programs, allowing donors to stand up new initiatives quickly and efficiently without needing to create a stand-alone nonprofit organization.

FIGURING OUT WHICH GIVING STRUCTURES MAKE THE MOST SENSE FOR YOU: KEY FUNCTIONAL QUESTIONS

There's a lot to consider as you try to figure out which giving structures are the best match for carrying out your giving. Here's what I recommend: begin by walking through whichever of the following functional questions are relevant to your giving, and then consult the corresponding sections of the summary chart at the end of this chapter (also available to download at the book's website). You'll still need to do your own diligence and consult your own financial and legal advisors before making your own decisions, but this chart is great for getting the big picture with a side-by-side view of the different features and attributes for the seven main structural options for your giving.

What: What Strategies Can You Carry Out?

Range of Recipients to Which You Can Give Charitable Grants

What's the issue here? Some giving structures, such as donor-advised funds, only allow you to give to entities that are established as public charities. You'll need to use a different structure if you want to make tax-deductible grants to individuals, such as for scholarships or for direct income support. This restriction also applies to any other entities that are not incorporated as public charities. For example, you cannot use a donor-advised fund to pay a consulting firm carrying out research related to your giving program.

Range of Recipients to Which You Can Give Noncharitable Grants

In some cases, your giving program might include supporting an activity that is not charitable. You might even have plans for things that are prohibited or limited for 501(c)(3) organizations, such as political campaign activity and certain kinds of issue advocacy. In many cases, donors simply engage in this kind of nondeductible giving by utilizing their personal funds. If you want to be able to carry out noncharitable giving through an organizational structure, you'll want to consider an LLC.

Ability to Operate Charitable Programs Directly

If you want to be able to create and run a charitable program that you finance yourself, it cannot be done on a tax-deductible basis out of your personal funds. This might seem strange, but there is no such thing as checkbook philanthropy when it comes to operating charitable programs yourself. Let's say you bought an RV, stocked it with books, and began using it to run an adult literacy program. You would not be able to treat these costs as tax-deductible charitable contributions. If you are planning to carry out programmatic activities yourself, you'll need to create a certain kind of organizational entity to do so. Private operating foundations are a common choice for this approach. In some cases, it may also be possible to do so through an LLC. Using an LLC confers a layer of liability protection between the donor/owner and the LLC's activities, but as a pass-through for tax purposes, an LLC's charitable programmatic expenses are not deductible to its owners. Another increasingly prevalent option is to seek a fiscal sponsor arrangement with an existing public charity, such as a community foundation, a well-established nonprofit in your field of interest, or a purpose-built sponsorship entity such as

New Venture Fund. In this case, you make a grant to the fiscal sponsor organization, and they administer the program under their auspices, usually charging an administrative fee for doing so. This arrangement allows you to test the waters with a new program without incurring the costs of forming an entity and seeking tax exemption.

Ability to Make Disbursements to Fulfill Personal Pledges

If a significant part of what you want to accomplish involves fulfilling personal pledges you've already made to support one or more charitable organizations, it's important to know that it's not permissible to make distributions from a donor-advised fund for this purpose. Similarly, you cannot use a private foundation to fulfill a personal pledge. However, it *is* permissible for the foundation itself to make and fulfill a pledge.

Ability to Give Anonymously

There might be a variety of reasons you'd like some or all of your giving to remain anonymous, from privacy concerns to religious beliefs. If anonymity is important to you, you'll want to consider this as you set up your philanthropic structures. Some vehicles, such as donor-advised funds and LLCs, make it easy to give anonymously. Others, like private foundations, require you to list your grant recipients and grant amounts in a publicly disclosed annual filing with the IRS.

Where: Where Are the Intended Recipients
of Your Giving Based?

Domestic vs. International Grantmaking

Individuals based in the United States cannot make tax-deductible contributions from personal funds to charitable organizations based overseas. In some cases, foreign charities have US-based "friends of" organizations that are eligible for US tax deductions. And if you operate a private foundation, you will have to undertake additional diligence requirements in order to disburse grants to non-US-based organizations. Similarly, if you are vesting resources in a donor-advised fund with the intention of giving overseas, it's important to make sure that the public charity that administers your DAF is prepared to take on these additional requirements. You may find that giving money to a philanthropic fund that specializes in international giving is an option you want to consider.

When: Over What Period of Time Do You
Intend to Conduct Your Giving?

Degree of Donor Family Control Over Time

Perhaps you're planning to give it all away in your own lifetime. Or, perhaps you intend to establish a giving program that carries on within your family over successive generations. Either way, the intended time period over which you want to disburse your resources and the degree of family control you want to maintain will have important implications for how you structure your giving. For example, the recommendation rights for a donor-advised fund can typically be passed on to one successive generation, whereas a private foundation can theoretically operate under your family's control in perpetuity—provided your descendants can agree to get along after you're gone!

Annual Distribution Requirements

This is a factor to consider if you want to have complete flexibility regarding how much you give away in any given year. For instance, private nonoperating foundations are required to give away at least 5 percent of their net assets each year. Conversely, donor-advised funds (as of this writing) have no annual distribution requirements. Some donors worry they won't be able to keep up with the 5 percent distribution requirement. This can be a particular concern if they are planning to vest large amounts of additional resources into their foundation in the future. In my experience, grantmaking quality does not actually appear to suffer in the struggle to keep up with the 5 percent requirement. There are a great many amazing organizations out there that are very much in need of support, and it only takes a little bit of outreach (often to other donors) to find them. Furthermore, there are some provisions that allow you a grace period to comply with the 5 percent requirement. If this is the main reason you are hanging back from creating a private foundation, this news should come as something of a relief; you likely don't need to worry so much about it.

Ability to Take Back Assets and Use Them for Other Charitable Purposes

What happens if you change your mind and want to restructure your giving down the road? Will you be able to take money that you've already vested within one type of entity and move it to another? Some vehicles, like LLCs, are very flexible in this regard because you don't get any charitable deduction upfront when you place resources in them. On the opposite end of the spectrum are donor-advised funds. Once you've claimed a charitable deduction by placing your money in a donor-advised fund, it's no longer "your" money, and you cannot get it back. In *theory*, you could impose certain restrictions on a gift to a donor-advised fund that would allow for you to recover funds under certain circumstances. These restrictions would be enforceable by authorities at the state level, but in practice most donor-advised funds won't accept restricted donations. The only thing you can do with this money is make recommendations for charitable grants to the public charity to whom these resources now belong. So, if you want to retain the ability to restructure your approach to giving down the road, it's crucial to keep this in mind.

Ability to Take Back Assets and Use Them for Noncharitable Purposes

How sure are you that you want to give these resources away? What if you change your mind and want to use them for some other purpose, like unexpected medical expenses or some other family emergency? If you want to have the ability to redirect your resources to noncharitable purposes later on, this is a crucial consideration to build into the structure of your giving. Once you've taken a tax deduction for placing your resources in any kind of charitable vehicle—whether a donor-advised fund or a private foundation—you can't take them back. The best you can generally do is move them from one charitable vehicle to another. So if you think that at some point you might need to reallocate resources to noncharitable purposes, an LLC might be the best option through which to carry out your giving. There's nothing irrevocable about putting your resources into an LLC because you are not eligible for a tax deduction until the moment the LLC itself makes charitable contributions.

Who: Who Is Involved in Distributing Your Giving?

Degree of Donor Control over an Entity's Governance

How much legal and practical control do you want to have over the governance of the entity in which you place your funds? The seven options we are reviewing here differ considerably regarding the extent to which you and your family members (or other related parties) can play a controlling role in governance. At one end of the spectrum, checkbook philanthropy and the solely owned LLC assure the donor the greatest degree of control. At the other end of the spectrum are donor-advised funds, which require you to give up legal and operational control in favor of the public charity to which you have given your funds. Although you do have the opportunity to make recommendations about grants to make with these funds, the DAF is under no legal obligation to follow your requests. In reality, the marketplace for DAFs is highly competitive. It is extremely unusual for a DAF not to honor such requests, provided the intended recipients are public charities in good standing.

Private foundations, including both nonoperating and operating varieties, show up much closer to the donor control side of the spectrum. You can form and operate these private foundations with no one other than you and your family members involved in their governance. As a consequence of this much donor control, private foundations face more restrictions and regulatory requirements than some of the other philanthropic vehicles. Other options, such as supporting organizations, sit in the middle of the donor control spectrum by providing the donor the opportunity to be represented on the governing board on a minority basis. In this case, the supported public charity takes the majority of seats. In practical terms, however, some donors have worked with donor-friendly public charities like community foundations to create supporting organizations. These can afford the donor a great deal of operational control on a day-to-day basis.

Compensation for Family Members and Related Parties

Do you want to be able to pay family members, business associates, and other related parties for serving on your board or for serving as staff? If so, you'll need to consider this as you structure your approach. Private foundations allow for this, meaning you can use dollars for which you have received a charitable tax deduction to pay family members and related parties a "reasonable" amount to compensate them for services rendered in governance or staffing roles. You can also compensate family members and related parties for services rendered to an LLC and, subject to some restrictions, treat these as deductible business expenses. Some other structures, such as DAFs, do not allow any compensation of family members or related parties.

Range of Unrelated Parties You Can Compensate for Services Rendered

If you expect to hire staff or consultants to help you carry out your giving, this is an important issue to consider. For example, if you vest all the resources you intend to use within a donor-advised fund and *then* decide you want to hire some help, you cannot use any resources from your donor-advised fund to pay for these staffing costs. This would leave you having to pay for staffing from your personal funds. But if you also have a private foundation or an LLC operating *alongside* your donor-advised fund, you may be able to treat staffing costs as the deductible operating expenses of these other entities.

Wealth Stock: What Forms of Wealth Do You Plan to Deploy in Your Giving?

Different Assets You Can Give to an Entity

If you have complex assets like artwork, real estate, or shares in closely held private companies that you want to use as the basis for your giving, then you'll need to consider what types of entities are able to receive or hold these assets. One important consideration is that private foundations cannot hold more than 20 percent of the voting shares in any one company. This is one reason Mark Zuckerberg and Priscilla Chan set up an LLC instead of a private foundation when they pledged to give away 99 percent of their majority interest of Facebook shares. This is definitely an area where you will want to seek expert guidance based on the assets you have in mind. For example, if you plan to donate complex assets to a donor-advised fund or philanthropic fund, you'll want to check with the administrators of those entities in advance regarding what range of assets they are equipped to accept or hold.

Another thing to consider is whether you plan to base your philanthropy on your own individual, intellectual, or social capital. If so, does this mean that you plan to run programs directly? Do you want to? As discussed under the "What" section previously, if you want to run programs directly, you may want to consider an LLC or private operating foundation to maximize your sense of involvement and fulfillment.

Whatever Else: Taxes, Financial Planning, Administrative Burden, Legal Liability, and More

Annual Tax-Deductibility Limits for Cash Gifts

The key distinction to track here is how much of your adjusted gross income (AGI) you can treat as a tax-deductible contribution to a giving vehicle each year. The limits vary and are subject to adjustment as policies change. In general, you can contribute 50–60 percent of your AGI in cash on a tax-deductible basis to a donor-advised fund. Conversely, the tax-deductible contribution limit for cash gifts to a private foundation is only 30 percent of your AGI in any given year. You may want to consider these limits when looking at your philanthropic structure if you are planning to make relatively large gifts as a percentage of your AGI each year.

Annual Tax-Deductibility Limits for Appreciated Assets

This is an issue if you want to donate appreciated securities, real estate, or other assets on which you have accumulated capital gains. Again, the tax-deductibility limits vary from one vehicle to the next, but in general, private foundations have a lower limit (20 percent of AGI) than do donor-advised funds (30 percent of AGI).

Tax Liability on Investment Earnings for Corporate Entities

Does it matter to you whether the entity you use to carry out your giving has ongoing tax obligations on income earned from its investments? This comes up particularly for private foundations, as they are generally liable to pay 2 percent of their net investment income in taxes on an annual basis. By contrast, donor-advised funds and supporting organizations operate as public charities. This means they are not generally subject to any tax obligation for earnings on investment income. This distinction is one reason some high-capacity donors who intend to actively manage their philanthropic resources for maximum investment return have created supporting organizations as the vehicle for doing so.

Degree of Donor Control Over Investment of Assets Held by Entities

If it's important to you to be able to closely manage the investment of the assets that form the basis for your giving, you'll want to consider this as you structure your giving. Generally speaking, the more closely you control the governance and operations of the entity, the more control you'll likely be able to have over the investment of its assets. This may be particularly important for donors who are investment professionals. There are certainly instances of private foundations whose investment performance dramatically outperforms the market due to the active engagement of the founder or other investment professionals serving on the board. The Lynch Foundation, for instance, would almost surely achieve better returns by having legendary stock picker Peter Lynch run its investment portfolio than it would parking its money in a typical mutual fund. That said, this isn't a decisive issue for many donors when making choices about how to structure their giving. Even donor-advised funds typically offer donors the opportunity to choose investment options from an array of risk-return profiles.

Administrative Burden, Including Annual Filing Requirements

How much does minimizing administrative burden matter to you? Some entities have virtually no administrative requirements on you as the donor. For example, donor-advised funds are administered entirely by the public charity with which the funds are vested. You can simply go online to see your fund balance, make contributions, adjust your investment allocations, and make grant recommendations. At the other end of the spectrum, private foundations have annual filing requirements with the IRS and potentially also with state authorities. It's worth noting that intermediaries like Foundation Source will handle most of the administrative requirements of running a private foundation for an annual fee, so you don't necessarily have to hire your own accountants and bookkeepers directly.

Liability Exposure

It's probably no surprise that your level of exposure to personal and/or organizational liability also varies considerably across the different giving structures. What kind of liability issues might come up in your giving? Good Samaritan laws provide some protection to individuals who engage in charitable activities in good faith when that activity somehow ends up resulting in injury or harm to others. Typically, the more control you have over the governance and operations, the more potential exposure you have to liability if something goes wrong. For example, if you establish a private foundation and serve on its board, you should carry directors and officers insurance. This provides liability protection for you and other board members from claims based on alleged wrongful acts by the corporation. If you give funds to a public charity to operate a donor-advised fund on your behalf, you typically won't have liability exposure. From a legal standpoint, you neither own nor control the resource in your donor-advised fund—any liability risk is assumed by the public charity operating the fund. As with so many other areas of your life, it makes sense to assess the risks of legal liability and proceed accordingly based on your own risk profile and preferences.

Fiduciary Duty Exposure

If you've ever been involved with corporate boards of publicly traded companies, you may be familiar with the notion that board members have a fiduciary duty to place the interests of share-holders first. The issue of fiduciary duty arises in philanthropic giving around the question of who holds the legal responsibility to act as a steward of any assets you place into vehicles commit-ted to charitable purposes. If you are operating as a checkbook philanthropist, the issue of fiduciary duty doesn't arise. However, as soon as you receive a tax deduction for contributing funds to a separate legal entity, the public has an interest in ensuring that those funds are used to provide public benefit. In turn, whoever runs that entity may have a legal duty to ensure that the orga-nization acts with appropriate care to steward those funds. As a cautionary tale, consider the court order that shut down the Donald J. Trump Foundation in 2019. Among the reasons for this action was that the organization had violated its fiduciary duty by using foundation funds to secure personal benefits for Donald Trump. One such expenditure was a six-foot-tall, $20,000 portrait of Trump paid for by the foundation and subsequently displayed in one of his golf properties.

CHARTING IT ALL OUT

There's a lot to keep track of here, so it may be helpful to have a visual aid. At the book's website you can find a chart that maps these functional design considerations across the seven different structures for carrying out your giving. Scan this QR code to see the detailed chart or visit www.moneywithmeaningbook.co.

Needless to say, this chart is not a definitive guide. You should also consult your own advisors and legal counsel as you determine which structures best meet your needs. Inevitably, there are trade-offs. It's quite possible that no single structure is going to be perfectly suited to meet all the design considerations that are important to you. This is why an increasing number of high-capacity donors are carrying out their giving through a combination of structural vehicles.

A Final Word on Taxes

All too often donors get tied up in knots trying to maximize their tax advantages. This is not a path to truly meaningful giving—not for you and not for the world. Why not view the tax treatment of your giving as merely one among many operational considerations? In other words, do what you can to maximize the resources available by getting the benefit of charitable tax deductions, but only when doing so doesn't distort your fundamental aims for impact or your sense of simplicity and personal fulfillment. After all, you are already planning to give this money away in pursuit of a better world. Why get hyper-focused on the intricacies of the tax code? If you wind up paying more taxes as you generate the greatest possible impact and personal joy, so be it!

Whatever design considerations are most important to you, none of them needs to be a barrier to gearing up your giving. Don't fall into the trap of senseless giving by holding back until you have the perfect structure. Simply getting started is often the best way to learn which structures will really make the most sense for your philanthropy in the long run.

SEEK AND SPEAK THE TRUTH

Tools for Better Thinking about Problems and Solutions

"Stop trying to change reality by eliminating complexity."

—DAVID WHYTE

A lot of philanthropy goes wrong by failing to reckon with reality. Donors can become so attached to their own vision and strategic plan that they end up trying to bend reality around themselves. Purposefully or not, they encourage those around them to voice only what they already want to hear. This has a terrible impact on their own effectiveness as donors. It can also be deeply dispiriting for their grantees and their staff.

Imagine if, as an investor in financial markets, you have a bedrock belief that the next wave of consumer demand in home furnishings is going to be all about sustainably sourced coconut fiber rugs and textiles. You and your family office investment team build up an elaborate investment thesis that includes positions in all the different layers of that supply chain, from coconut groves to fiber processing plants. Every time your team brings you the latest data showing that nobody actually wants to buy anything made with coconut fiber, you tell them there must be something wrong with their measurements, or you insist the breakthrough is just around the corner. Even with really deep pockets, chances are you won't be able to sustain your coconut-fiber bet against the reality of the global commodities market for very long.

In many philanthropic arenas, there is no similar forcing mechanism that requires you to objectively evaluate the evidence and reckon with the world as it actually is. After all, you are trying to change how the world "actually" is with your philanthropy, right? As long as you have money to give away, you can keep right on doing something that is not only out of touch with reality but may even be actively harmful. Take, for example, New York City financier Bernard Selz and his wife Lisa. They have devoted millions of dollars over many years to support the anti-vaccination movement, spreading disinformation in the midst of localized measles outbreaks in New York city and beyond.[14]

This is why it is so important to seek and speak the truth to everyone—including yourself—as you gear up your giving. If you want to uphold this commitment, there are several modes of thinking that will really help. These ways of thinking are important tools for getting real about how you focus your philanthropy: systems thinking, critical thinking, and design thinking.

If the issues that matter most to you are complex, systems thinking equips you with a framework for making sense of the multifaceted mess. It's about getting all the way down to the root causes of the problems you care about. This is especially important for spotting feedback loops and unintended consequences that can derail your plans despite your best intentions.

Speaking of messy reality, there's a whole lot of sloppy thinking in the world of philanthropy. Critical thinking is a key antidote. If you're going to be the one making consequential decisions about how to allocate your philanthropic resources, the quality of your reasoning process really matters! This includes your ability to overcome (or at least identify) your own blind spots and cognitive biases. This is especially important when grappling with issues of race, power, and identity. Having the discipline to step up your game as a critical thinker is a great way to step up your effectiveness as a philanthropist.

Finally, ensuring that the people closest to the problem have a full voice in developing the solutions is one of the foundations of meaningful giving. This requires design thinking. For example, if your goal was to save honeybees from hive die-offs in California's almond country, you'd spend a lot of time talking with commercial beekeepers and the farmers who depend on them—you wouldn't just hire a newly minted PhD with an intriguing theory and let them have at it.

What if you have already made the decision that your joy and your impact is best served by delegating decision-making authority over your giving to someone else with more time and proximity to the issues you care most about? In that case, you might not need to worry so much about applying systems thinking, critical thinking, and design thinking on a day-to-day basis. However, it's still important to be familiar with these three modes of thought; doing so will better equip you to fully appreciate the deeper impacts of your giving over time and inspire you to focus your resources where they can truly do the most good.

THE REAL WORLD DOESN'T CARE WHAT YOUR THEORY OF CHANGE PREDICTS

Sometimes in life—and all too often in philanthropy—the best intentions have unanticipated consequences. One of the staples in the global campaign to eradicate malaria has been philanthropic funding for millions of bed nets. These bed nets have reduced the incidence of malaria and saved lives. So, there's no such thing as too many bed nets, right? Unfortunately, there is growing evidence that in some places, free bed nets have become so plentiful that they are finding an unanticipated alternative use as fishing nets. These have the potential to do significant ecological damage. Because bed nets are designed to keep mosquitoes out, their super-small mesh means they succeed in harvesting even the smallest and youngest fish when used for fishing. This is causing local fish populations to crash. People then use the bed nets to fish even more intensively, chasing a disappearing resource.[15]

Stories like these are a reminder that no matter how lofty our vision or admirable our goals, meaningful giving requires that we work hard to understand the complex interconnectivity of the systems we are seeking to "fix."

Without a deep understanding of what's real—of how the complicated systems we seek to improve *actually* function, particularly around dynamics of power, community, race, and identity—we cannot be sure that our solutions are the right ones or are truly moving things in a positive direction. In the worst-case scenario, these solutions may even produce more harm than good. When we fail to get real as agents of change, we are failing ourselves and everyone else who participates in the systems we seek to change. To maximize our chances of making lasting positive change, we must do everything we can to understand how these systems actually work and what our own role is in them.

Systems thinking, critical thinking, and design thinking help donors looking to grapple with complex realities develop constructive paths forward. Through my years as a philanthropy advisor, I have found that donors with the deepest commitment to tackling tough challenges tend to draw on one or more of these three modes of thought. Each helps provide a window into seeing the world as it actually is, and together, they offer even more clarity. Systems thinking is an essential tool to better understand the world around you and the systems whose outcomes you are seeking to improve. Critical thinking is a vital tool to better understand yourself, your perspective, your identity, and your own role in the deeper systems and structures you are seeking to change. Design thinking is a key way to develop solutions that are most likely to stick. This is because they are designed in partnership with those closest to the problem itself; they are designed around meeting the needs that they themselves have identified as most pressing.

The most effective donors use these tools as a matter of course. By doing so, they also make straightforward, nonideological conversations about race, equity, diversity, and identity a building block for better giving rather than an afterthought.

TOOL 1: SYSTEMS THINKING

The term "systems thinking" was coined by Barry Richmond of MIT in the late 1980s. It was made popular a few years later by Peter Senge in his bestselling business management book *The Fifth Discipline*. Systems thinking focuses on breaking down systems into three elements. These are the components of the system, the interconnections between the components in the system, and the outcomes reliably produced by the system. In other words, the system's real, functional results, regardless of whatever its stated purpose is supposed to be.

Systems thinking is often represented by causal loop diagrams. These graphics provide a visual representation of how the components of a system are interconnected and how feedback loops influence the performance of a system over time. Here's an advanced example of systems thinking applied to the interactions of fishing and other human activity with global fishery stocks.

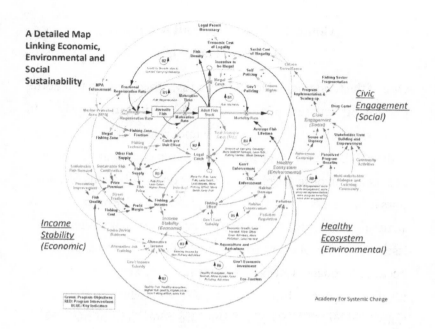

A Detailed Map Linking Economic, Environmental and Social Sustainability

Reproduced with permission from Joe Hsueh,
Academy for Systemic Change

If you are trained to build and read these kinds of diagrams, there's a powerful and counterintuitive story here about how to manage fisheries as a common resource. Unfortunately, for many of us, the symbolic notation and fine print of formal systems mapping is hard to follow. But never fear—systems thinking isn't just a tool for specialists. In this chapter we'll walk through a simple and straightforward way of using systems thinking as you gear up your giving.

Complex Systems Are All Around Us,
Hiding in Plain Sight

One of the fundamental ideas behind systems thinking is that the underlying structure of a system is often hiding in plain sight. In other words, we can figure out the underlying structure because it drives the behavior of the system. This comes in the form of events we can observe, playing out over time. As Donella Meadows puts it in her excellent book, *Systems Thinking: A Primer*, "System structure is the source of system behavior. System behavior reveals itself as a series of events over time." She goes on to explain that because language occurs in a linear fashion, words aren't always ideal descriptors. Unlike forming a linear, logical sentence, systems happen all at once, and they are connected in many ways. This is also why it can be useful to reference visuals that allow us to "see" the system components and their interconnections. Visual representations enable us to conceive of the system as a whole, empowering us to develop a better understanding of why it ends up producing the outcomes that it does. This is something that even a completely thorough, sequential narrative cataloging every system component and interconnection doesn't allow us to do. The mapping approach also lets us see the construction of the larger system. It may be made up of different subsystems, sometimes with competing aims. This is very important when we are looking for deeper insight into how a system's underlying structure drives outcomes in the form of visible behavior and events.

Looking at the whole picture can be particularly important when a system's actual outcomes are consistently different from its stated aims or intended purpose. For example, employers with a policy of not hiring convicted felons are presumably seeking to make their own places of employment safer. State policymakers enacting "three strikes and you're out" felony laws, mandating lifetime imprisonment without parole, are supposedly also seeking to protect public safety. But taken together, these policies can create circumstances in which someone with two criminal convictions and few prospects for gainful employment has the path back to prison already paved for them—a terrible outcome for them, as well as any victims of their third offense.

Our Brains Don't Naturally Work This Way

Systems thinking is challenging because we are wired to look at the world in simpler terms. Linear, event-focused, cause-and-effect thinking is our go-to mental strategy for making sense of the world around us. Clearly, the linear approach has served humanity well over many thousands of years. The thing is, straightforward rules of cause and effect work just fine until they don't. As our societies have become increasingly complex and interconnected, we need to develop new tools to understand the deeper structures that drive events. Systems thinking helps us understand how our own actions play out over time across the complex social, economic, and political systems we have created. For instance, Newton's three laws of motion are straightforward and useful, but Newtonian physics simply cannot account for, calculate, or assess some of the latest complex revelations about the universe. Quantum physics offers a much better view and enables us to keep moving, advancing, and succeeding in this area. Just as we still use Newton's laws to calculate satellite-launch trajectories, we are now looking to and learning about quantum physics to help us sort out the dynamics governing the complex relationships among subatomic particles.

How do you know when you need systems thinking? Here are five circumstances to watch for:

1. When we continue to have problems in spite of our best efforts to address them over an extended period of time

2. When unintended consequences seem to be proliferating

3. When linear cause-and-effect models don't lead to the expected results

4. When a situation is too complex for us to remember all the pieces and their interconnections

5. When the actual results of an institution or social system are consistently different from its stated goals or purpose

It's worth remembering that complex systems can be at play in seemingly mundane areas of daily life, like whether our favorite brand of beer is going to be in stock at the local store. Harvard Business School has a case study called "The Beer Game" that is famous among supply-chain geeks. This case shows just how counterintuitive and unpredictable systems dynamics can be in a simple supply chain. In the example, a package store owner and a brewery sales manager are the only players. Due to delays between placing orders to the brewery for more beer and actually receiving the beer at the package store, it is remarkably hard for players to maintain a stable equilibrium between supply and demand. This simulated game frequently results in wild swings between drastic shortages and massive oversupplies of beer following even small changes in consumer demand week to week. The more interconnected and complex our world becomes, the more it becomes full of systems whose behavior defies our instincts for straightforward, linear, cause-and-effect relationships. That's a lot more going on behind the scenes than most of us are thinking about when we reach for a cold one. It can be much the same thing when donors say, "There's clearly a shortage of X in the community! Let's order up some more…"

When You Engage with the System, You Become Part of It

By helping to illuminate deeper systems at play, unexpected feedback loops, and other counterintuitive dynamics, systems thinking helps us gain clarity as change agents. This is a matter not of subscribing to ideologically driven articles of faith but rather of pragmatic reflection on how the systems around us actually function, whatever their stated purpose. For instance, for a donor hoping to drive social change, it is especially important to consider the following:

- You do not exist as an independent actor within the system you are seeking to engage. *When you engage with a system, you become part of that system*—a component of the system who has an interconnected relationship with its other components.

- When we set aside our ideological lenses and step back to examine existing systems of public education, criminal justice, public health, and others, the data suggests that whatever their stated intent, *these systems have, in practice, reliably produced outcomes in which people of color, poor people, and a variety of other groups have been consistently disadvantaged.*

- Even if you don't think of yourself as having any prior role in the system whose unequal outcomes you are trying to change, there's a strong possibility that when you fully map out the components, interconnectivity, and subsystems, you'll find that *you are indeed playing some role.* Most of these systems are so broad and deep that we almost can't help but participate, however unwillingly or unintentionally. For example, in making our own choices about which neighborhoods to live in and which schools our children will attend, we are often participating in the very system of geographic zoning for housing and school attendance that consistently replicates poor outcomes for other people's children.

Root Cause Analysis:
A Practical Way to Apply Systems Thinking

One reason systems thinking isn't used more widely already is that the tools for applying it have often been presented in a very dense, challenging fashion. Remember the fishery loop diagram from a few pages ago? There's deep insight there, but it looks a lot like a bowl of spaghetti to the untrained eye. Learning to understand, much less construct, the causal loop diagrams presented in systems-thinking textbooks is much like learning a new language. It can be very rewarding, but nobody pretends it's easy. Let's walk through a simple, straightforward approach that you can use on a practical basis with just a fraction of the time and effort required to master formal systems mapping. This step-by-step guide seeks to provide a clear and practical process that can be applied both by individuals and by groups working together.[16]

1. Begin by brainstorming ways to define the problem in terms of a consistent outcome that you and other key stakeholders *don't* want. Here we are using systems thinking, but we are starting with the system's outputs first. We are not worrying about trying to list all its components or their interconnections at this time. This is often the simplest way to begin understanding how a system works at a holistic level. Indeed, the best place to start when engaging with any system is carefully observing its actual behavior rather than watching for what it is "supposed" to do.

2. Evaluate the list of brainstormed problems, and determine which one comes closest to the thing you are really trying to resolve and improve. At this stage, you want to look for the root problem; you are looking for something your philanthropic efforts can fix that will unlock a cascade of benefits and will *not* immediately create new problems. Also, express the problematic outcome you have identified in "human-centered" terms—how is this negative outcome expressed in terms of the experience of those closest to the problem?

3. Now it's time to get to the whiteboard. Right in the middle, write out the root problem statement as a sentence with both a noun and a verb, and draw a box around it. For example: *The number of students in our state who are able to attend innovative, safe, and engaging schools that they love barely grows each year, while the number of students who attend unsafe, boring, and substandard schools that they have no emotional attachment to remains persistently high.*

4. Read the sentence you just drew a box around, and ask yourself why this is happening and what the cause is. Write the first answer that comes to mind as a sentence with a noun and a verb. Put a box around it, and draw an arrow from the first box to the second one. Now, look at the second box again, and ask yourself why *this* is happening. What is the deeper cause? What is the deeper cause of *this* deeper cause?

5. Keep drilling down, recording your answers. Do this at least five times to get as far down to the bedrock issue as you can. You will likely notice that as you progress, you identify some "whys," You may even discover the root problem itself in a feedback loop. This is shown in upward looping arrows in the example diagram below. This is a good thing because feedback loops are powerful places on which to focus your intervention in a system.

6. As this map begins to take shape, start looking for individuals or entities who seem to come up repeatedly or in multiple boxes. Keep a running list of all the nouns (individuals and entities) who are playing roles as actors in the answers to your successive *whys*. In systems-thinking language, these are the "components" of the system.

7. Keep track of the verbs that show up in your boxes. In systems-thinking language, these are the clues to the "interconnections" of the system. If you were making a formal causal loop diagram, there would be only nouns in your boxes. Verbs allow you to explicitly narrate key actions and interconnections that drive the system's behavior, and they substitute for all kinds of specialized symbols that are used in a formal systems map.

8. Very often, you can gain significant insight into promising leverage points for intervening in a system simply by sketching it out on a whiteboard. You can now "see"

significant elements or even the whole thing all at once. This is a big upgrade from trying to tell yourself the story just with words. Looking at this emerging sketch, you are now better positioned to choose a point of leverage. Disrupting feedback loops is one powerful way to get a system to behave differently. Another way to maximize your leverage is to intervene as close as possible to the root cause. This way, you won't need to worry as much about intermediating factors diluting the positive force of your intervention.

Below is an example of this method, applied to the root problem statement: "High-quality, student-centered new schools grow slowly while low-quality schools easily persist." Starting with this problem statement and asking why multiple times eventually leads to factors that loop back up to help explain the problem statement itself. There's a good chance you can find powerful systemic leverage points related to whatever is in the boxes where the feedback arrows originate, or even a step or two below them in the chain of *whys*.

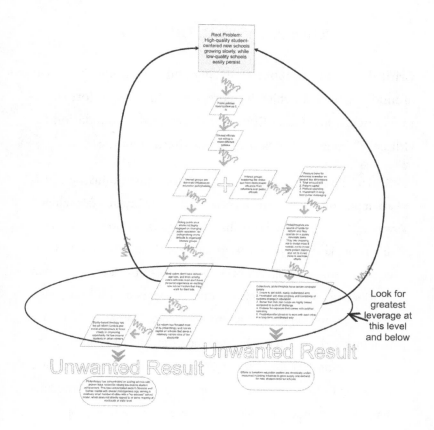

Root-cause analysis can be a very powerful and relatively quick way to put the tools of systems thinking to work for you, but it isn't infallible. First, the results of a root-cause analysis exercise *are only as good as your reasoning*. So, reason carefully, and be honest. It is often helpful to write out the assumptions you are making at each step and pressure test them for plausibility. Likewise, root-cause analysis can lead you astray if you're not wary of your own blind spots, groupthink, and other cognitive biases. This is why we turn next to stepping up our critical thinking skills!

TOOL 2: CRITICAL THINKING

Critical thinking is about analyzing and evaluating the world around you from an objective perspective in order to form accurate conclusions. Linda Elder, President of the Foundation for Critical Thinking, defines critical thinking as follows:

> Critical thinking is self-guided, self-disciplined thinking which attempts to reason at the highest level of quality in a fair-minded way... [Critical thinkers] realize that no matter how skilled they are as thinkers, they can always improve their reasoning abilities and they will at times fall prey to mistakes in reasoning, human irrationality, prejudices, biases, distortions, uncritically accepted social rules and taboos, self-interest, and vested interest. They strive to improve the world in whatever ways they can and contribute to a more rational, civilized society. At the same time, they recognize the complexities often inherent in doing so. They avoid thinking simplistically about complicated issues and strive to appropriately consider the rights and needs of relevant others. They recognize the complexities in developing as thinkers, and commit themselves to lifelong practice toward self-improvement. They embody the Socratic principle: The unexamined life is not worth living, because they realize that many unexamined lives together result in an uncritical, unjust, dangerous world.[17]

The more you are drawn to address complex social challenges in your giving, the more critical thinking becomes key. Critical thinking can be particularly valuable when you apply it to yourself as a donor. Ask yourself, "What are my blind spots, filters, and cognitive biases, and how can I work around the limits of my own perspective to maximize my impact?" It is an essential tool for unpacking issues of power, identity, and race, particularly if you are a member of a historically dominant cultural group. For example, it's hard to fully evaluate the concept of "whiteness" in a nonideological way without drawing on the tools of critical thinking.

So, what does critical thinking entail on a practical basis? How do we implement it as part of our tool kit for getting real? A relatively straightforward way to get at this is through the PERC framework presented below. This approach breaks critical thinking down into four basic components: purpose, evidence, reasoning, and conclusions.

PERC Framework for Critical Thinking

Purpose: You begin by explicitly stating the objective of the critical-thinking process. What are you seeking to achieve through the application of critical thinking? What question are you seeking to answer, and what issue are you trying to understand?

Evidence: The next step is to seek out and organize the evidence that relates to the question at hand. As you determine what to consider in your reasoning process, it is vital to distinguish between two distinct types of decision-making inputs:

- **Objective evidence**: Facts and information that can be independently evaluated and empirically proven. You are entitled to your own opinion but not to your own facts.

- **Subjective opinion**: Preconceptions, assumptions, beliefs, and biases that the thinker is bringing to the table. These must be either accepted or rejected as a matter of opinion—they cannot be empirically proven.

At first, it might seem like critical thinking is about setting aside subjective opinion and drawing solely on objective evidence. However, a truly sophisticated critical thinker does not focus only on immediately verifiable, empirical facts. For one thing, doing so may not sufficiently account for the emotionally driven reactions of others within a complex system. Great critical thinkers must consider subjective opinions in themselves and others. Your goal is to figure out how the feelings, beliefs, biases, and habitual mental shortcuts of all those involved influence the matter at hand. Sometimes, it's even possible to gather objective evidence about subjective feelings. We see this with polling, focus groups, and other opinion-research techniques.

Reasoning Process: Now we come to the part of the process where you are assembling the evidence as pieces of a puzzle. Let's stick with this metaphor for a moment. When you are putting together puzzles, it's common practice to look for the edge pieces first. This creates the frame in which all the other pieces must fit. The illustration on the box of the puzzle is an even more powerful frame. It tells you what the big picture will actually look like after you have successfully fit all the pieces together. Frames are very powerful devices when it comes to our reasoning process. They can lead us to profound insight, but they can also lead us astray. Imagine trying to do a puzzle after someone switched up the cover picture on you. This leads us to several key elements of the reasoning process:

- State your framing of the situation explicitly, and identify at least two alternative ways you could frame the same context. For example:
  - "The glass is half full."
  - "The glass is half empty."
  - "The atmospheric conditions here allow for liquid at room temperature."
- Critically evaluate your choice of frames. Consider which aspects of the situation your framing emphasizes and which it de-emphasizes. Does the medical treatment under consideration save 80 percent of patients, or does it fail to save 20 percent of patients? An 80 percent survival rate and a 20 percent mortality rate are logically equivalent, but the framing is quite different. Framing may also contain subtle clues about the previous context. For example, "The glass is half full" might suggest it was less full previously, whereas "The glass is half empty" might suggest it was more full before.[18]
  - Use inference (step-by-step, logical reasoning) to connect the relevant, objective information in a logical way to make the best possible educated guess with the available information.
  - Step back and ask yourself how your subjective opinions and perspective might influence your reasoning.

○ Make sure you have sufficiently accounted for the subjective opinions of others and any of their known mental processes in your own reasoning. Are you overly reliant on assumptions that the behaviors of others will be shaped by rational, objective factors?

Conclusions: Once your reasoning produces a conclusion (e.g., your best possible educated guess), it's vital to critically evaluate this conclusion itself. Ask yourself, "So what?" Just because you have produced an insight through a logical reasoning process doesn't necessarily mean it has bearing on the original question you set out to answer. If you forget this step, you may find yourself getting distracted by irrelevant logic chains. For example, let's say my original purpose for engaging in critical thinking is to figure out why my car won't start. First, I diligently review the evidence: little mouse droppings, rips in my upholstery, and that tail I briefly glimpsed disappearing behind the dashboard. Then, I engage in my reasoning process, concluding that I've got a pernicious case of vehicular mice. This logical conclusion may be perfectly correct, but without additional evidence, this is *not necessarily* the reason my car won't start.

Improving Critical Thinking

At each step of the critical-thinking process there is the potential for error. Strong critical thinkers reduce the incidence of error at each of these levels by following these best practices:

1. **Establish your purpose thoughtfully and explicitly.**
   If you aren't asking a question or examining an issue
   with the potential to inform the outcomes you really
   care about, you are already in trouble.

2. **Gather accurate information and facts.** Work hard
   to supplement available facts when you start out
   with too little information to form reliable, informed
   conclusions.

3. **Be aware of and account for subjective preconceptions (conscious and unconscious).** Identify and
   appropriately discount biases, assumptions, beliefs,
   opinions, heuristics (mental shortcuts), and other rules
   of thumb. It is crucial that you do not mistake your own
   subjective preconceptions for objective facts. Another
   hallmark of strong critical thinking is the capacity to
   appreciate and account for the role these preconceptions have in shaping the behavior of all those involved.
   Not every preconception is automatically wrong. Certain
   "rules of thumb" actually have lots of valid historical
   experience backing them up. They are highly functional
   shortcuts for our brains, and they work the vast majority of the time. Just because someone is not applying
   rigorous logical reasoning in the moment does not mean
   they are acting illogically. For example, think about
   looking both ways before crossing a street. Now, imagine
   that the street has been closed to all traffic for a street
   fair. It is a lot of work to switch on our critical-thinking

faculties and override our instinct to look both ways. Over millennia of evolution, we have been wired to take shortcuts whenever the error rate for doing so is acceptably low. That said, leaving our critical faculties switched off and letting our brains run on autopilot is also the source of some of our trickiest cognitive biases.

4. **Be thoughtful and compassionate about how these preconceptions influence all of us.**

5. **Be intentional about your framing.** Spot hidden frames, and understand how framing fundamentally shapes your logical process and conclusions. Try on different frames to see if they lead you to different conclusions.

6. **Be rigorous and methodical in inferential reasoning.** Look for places in your logic chain where magical thinking is entering in. In other words, make sure you aren't making unfounded assumptions or leaps in reasoning that aren't supported by the available facts. Use Occam's razor—more memorably stated as, "Keep it simple, stupid!"

7. **Be self-reflective about your conclusions.** It is helpful to ask yourself, "And how would I feel if I had reached the opposite conclusion? Is it possible that my feelings about this conclusion influenced the process I used to reach this conclusion? What other conclusions might I reach if I approached this issue from a different angle?"

8. **Engage in a post-reasoning relevance check.** Reflect on why this actually matters regarding the issue you initially

identified. If the conclusion you just reached is true, what difference does it make in the world? Beyond the immediate implications, what are the second- and third-order effects? This is an instance where systems thinking and root-cause analysis can be really helpful.

TOOL 3: DESIGN THINKING

Design thinking helps you develop new approaches for working creatively with others, including those who are closest to the problems you are seeking to solve. IDEO and other cutting-edge design firms have pioneered the concept of "user experience" (UX) and "human-centered design." These ideas are rapidly moving beyond the Silicon Valley startup scene and into the mainstream. The design-thinking approach is a great complement to systems thinking and critical thinking. Doing it well requires that you get beyond the limitations of your own vantage point. This can be particularly important for all of us who typically operate in the mode of "rational experts." If you are pretty sure everything would work out great in your giving if you could just convince the rest of the world to see things your way, that's reason enough to consider design thinking!

The Five Stages of Design Thinking

The Institute of Design at Stanford University, otherwise known as the "d.school" has generated much of the intellectual capital behind the design-thinking approach as it is practiced at firms like IDEO. There are five stages in the d.school's model for design thinking.

1. **Empathize**: This involves working as closely as possible with those who are closest to the challenge or problem in question. This is about getting real by understanding their interests, needs, desires, and unique experiences of the world as it actually plays out for them. This step also draws on your critical-thinking skills. The more you can set aside your own preconceptions and assumptions about how the world works, the better able you will be to appreciate the experience of those who are most directly impacted by whatever challenge you are seeking to tackle. Even if you consider yourself to be a stakeholder who is very much among those directly impacted by the issue at hand, it is still valuable to engage others with a variety of perspectives to make sure you have the fullest possible picture of what's "real." This is where sayings about the "wisdom of the group" and "many minds are better than one" come into their own. For example, this is exactly what the Geraldine R. Dodge Foundation has done by sponsoring focus groups for local nonprofit media organizations to learn more about what their readers and listeners actually want and need when it comes to coverage of local news.

2. **Define**: This involves synthesizing all the information and perspectives you have gathered from those

closest to the problem. The goal is to define the issue in human-centered terms. This is a great stage in which to apply the root-cause analysis tool. Generate a single-sentence problem statement in which those closest to the issue play the starring role. For example, instead of defining the problem they are working to solve as "universal access to high-quality preschool," here's how the Trust For Learning lays out the issue instead: "Our work is to make sure that every child has access to high-quality early learning that meets them where they are, prepares them for success in school, and takes them where they want to be in life."

3. **Ideate**: With a human-centered problem statement in hand, it's time to get creative. Given our deeper understanding of what those with the greatest proximity to the problem are experiencing, it's time to ask how we might incorporate innovative approaches, features, and attributes into a new design that will make this user experience markedly better. Unusual brainstorming techniques can be helpful here. One example is the "Worst Possible Idea" game. Participants get their creative process flowing by trying to come up with ideas that they are sure would be a giant step backward and then flip them around to look for unusual paths toward improvement.

4. **Prototype**: The idea here is to take promising ideas generated during the ideation stage and test them with end users as quickly as possible. This is how RevX, a

project of Transcend Education, works with students to test out potential solutions to learning-design problems that the students themselves identify. After students at one participating school in Edgecombe County, North Carolina, decided they wanted to focus on ideas that would make their playground more inclusive for students with mobility challenges, they tested out an idea by working together to build a small, raised-garden bed in one area of the playground. "Failing fast" is a virtue here. It's far better to get early information about what works and what doesn't with the people whose needs we are ultimately seeking to satisfy. You want to avoid investing lots of time and resources on a dead end.

5. **Test:** Now it's time to test the most promising potential solutions in a much more rigorous fashion. Again, the needs and perspectives of those closest to the problem are paramount. You also want to use systems-thinking and critical-thinking skills to look for unintended consequences and feedback loops, as well as for blind spots that might be obscuring the vision. The goal is to develop a solution that has the greatest likelihood of actually delivering the results you intend out in the real world.

It's important to note that applying the five stages of design thinking is not typically a linear process. Even when we reach Stage Five and test a solution that appears to be successful, our work is never fully done because we know we are engaging in a dynamic systems process. The good news is that if your solution stops working or needs adjustment, you can simply return to the design-thinking process and begin modifying it to produce better results. Often, it will make sense to be engaged on multiple steps simultaneously, toggling back and forth among them as you go. The five-step framework is useful to make sure that however you go about it, you cover these steps as part of your process.

USING THESE TOOLS TO GET REAL ABOUT RACE, DIVERSITY, EQUITY, AND IDENTITY

No matter who you are, but especially if you are white or otherwise experience the world through the lens of a dominant cultural group, it makes sense to think about race, equity, diversity, and identity *before* you intervene in the system, not as an afterthought. Although the public conversation on these topics has become increasingly polarized, for donors who want to maximize the impact of their giving, this is a practical matter, not an ideological one. Systems thinking and critical thinking can help you consciously set aside your preconceived ideas and ideology and focus on the careful thought and discipline it takes to do systems-change work effectively. And design thinking is a key way to understand what is real for those at the heart of the system you are interested in improving—allowing creative solutions to emerge that are truly responsive to those needs.

So, whatever your own ideological starting point as a donor, there are a few points to keep in mind as you bring these tools to bear around key issues of race, identity, and power. First, as donors, we should not be surprised—much less offended—when those we are seeking to help have questions about our motives. People who have been continuously disadvantaged by a system's consistent replication of inequality over a long period of time may wonder where we've been all this time. Even if we insist on seeing ourselves as outsiders to the system we are trying to change, the people within the system will likely have no such illusions. People within the system may also wonder why we are not showing up to address inequality in other social arenas that are systematically producing equally bad results for them. For example, why are some of us only showing up on the issue of education reform but not criminal justice reform or affordable housing? Further, we should be ready to back the wisdom and judgment of those with greater proximity to the system and its negative impacts. This doesn't mean we have to completely abandon our own ideas for making change, but it does mean we should not assume we already have the answers when it comes to identifying the most promising levers for shifting that system.

The world is more complex than ever, so seeing this world as it truly is *requires* more of us than ever. As a donor committed to giving that makes sense, you must draw on the best tools, techniques, and technologies for getting real.

8

ASSESSING IMPACT

What to Measure and Why It Matters

> *"If you think you know how much impact might flow from acting on any of your own impulses to give, you are almost certainly wrong..."*
>
> —MACKENZIE SCOTT

One of the most common concerns donors raise when preparing to gear up their giving is whether or not their money is actually making a difference. It's one of the primary reasons so much money is sitting on the sidelines in philanthropy. As the amount of money you give increases, you may no longer feel satisfied simply writing a check and hoping for the best. That's understandable. Whatever the scale of your giving, chances are it took a lot of time and energy to accumulate the resources you now want to share with the world. It's easy to feel like it would be irresponsible not to have some way of assessing impact and then directing resources accordingly. You don't want your money to be squandered, and you don't want it to be just another drop in a bottomless bucket of nonprofit fundraising.

That said, assessing the true impact of your giving is tricky. There are unintended consequences and lots of opportunity to lose the thread of meaningful giving. It's easy to run afoul of the four commitments of meaningful giving when it comes to measuring impact. Take, for example, the donor who complains to an advocacy organization:

*"You are taking credit for others' work.
This advocacy campaign was a coalition effort,
and you weren't solely responsible for the outcomes.
We want to understand how the money we gave you
produced a truly distinct impact—otherwise, it seems
like we are funding all of you to do the same things
and fight with each other to take credit."*

The donor might be correct in a narrow sense, but the organization's leader could just as easily reply:

*"You aren't the only funder supporting this work, and your
money is blended together across all these organizations.
So, in fact, none of us can uniquely attribute impact to
our own organization or to a specific donor's grant."*

What happens next? Very often, the organization doesn't want to risk their funding in a dispute with a donor. So, they give the donor what they're asking for. They put their development and communications team to work crafting a story for the donor about how uniquely impactful their support is. They tell this story at the expense of the complex and collaborative teamwork it actually takes to make progress on the issue that both they and the donor care deeply about. And in the process they make it harder for that advocacy coalition to collaborate effectively in the future.

You can find a different and better way to understand the impact of your giving. We will break down this topic into four key questions and give you a practical framework for handling this important challenge as you gear up your giving.

1. What are the psychological benefits of assessing impact?

2. What is your practical purpose for assessing impact?

3. How do you define impact? What is the causal mechanism for achieving impact on the issue you're focused on? How tightly linked are the causal chains between your actions as a donor, the work of your grantees, and the ultimate outcomes you all care about? And how much control do your funding recipients have over the ultimate outcomes?

4. What kind of "impact appetite" do you have as a donor? Are you an attribution maximizer or a contribution maximizer?

PSYCHOLOGICAL BENEFITS OF
ASSESSING IMPACT

We've already talked about strategic philanthropy—giving in which you engage strategically to maximize your contribution's positive social impact. This is a laudable goal, and it's easy to see why this is a standard on which so many philanthropists set their sights. Almost every cultural tradition emphasizes that the most important objective of giving is to benefit others. But as we explored in Chapter 1, meaningful giving is not only about maximizing the positive social benefit of your giving; it is also about giving in a way that you find personally fulfilling. If you truly aspire to maximize the impact of your giving and its benefit for others, you *must* conduct your giving in a way that you find personally gratifying as well. Otherwise, you run a grave risk of underperforming: giving less in financial terms and giving less of your time and attention. Don't let your philanthropy end up feeling like a chore you'd rather put off. This is why it's so important to be clear with yourself about how measuring your impact as a donor connects to your currency of fulfillment.

There are several ways that being able to assess the impact of your giving can help you feel fulfilled. This is where it's helpful to remember the framework of human needs psychology that we discussed in Chapter 2: the seven innate human drives at the center of your psychological system.

Recall that, in this framework, we are distinguishing between four lower-level, ego-driven needs and three higher-level, self-actualizing drives. Measuring the impact of your giving can help you meet both kinds of needs. On the lower-level side, knowing exactly what the impact of your giving is helps you meet the need for security and certainty. So, too, with your need for novelty—the process of measuring impact can provide a thrill of suspense as you figure out whether your investment paid off or not. Because impact is valued as a major status symbol in strategic philanthropy, being able to measure the impact of your giving can help you meet your need for social status and significance. Measuring impact also helps you meet higher-level, self-actualizing needs. Clearly, knowing that your giving has produced a positive impact can help you meet your need for social contribution. The challenge of the measurement process also creates an opportunity for personal learning and growth.

As we've just reviewed, from a psychological standpoint, there are quite a few reasons you are likely to care about knowing the impact of your giving. This is why measuring impact is central to many donors' currency of fulfillment. It's perfectly fine to have lower-level psychological needs in play when it comes to assessing the impact of your giving. However, if these lower-level psychological needs (certainty, novelty, social status, and social connection) are the primary reason you are focused on measuring impact, you run the risk of slipping into selfish giving. This is what happens when you are indulging in ego gratification at the expense of giving that maximizes both impact and long-term fulfillment.

WHAT IS YOUR PRACTICAL PURPOSE
FOR ASSESSING IMPACT?

Understanding the ultimate impact of your giving might be psychologically important, but when it comes to meaningful giving, it's equally important to consider the practical purposes of impact assessment.

There are at least three ways that impact assessment can inform your decisions as a donor. First, you can use impact data to better inform your choice of philanthropic focus, leading you to allocate more resources to those issues where your giving is showing the greatest impact. Second, you can act on this data for purposes of grantee selection. Finally, you can draw on this data to help grantees with performance improvement.

Let's walk through these three decision-making points. Take stock of your cross-cutting commitments as you consider the role of impact assessment in your giving.

Three Key Impact-Driven Decisions

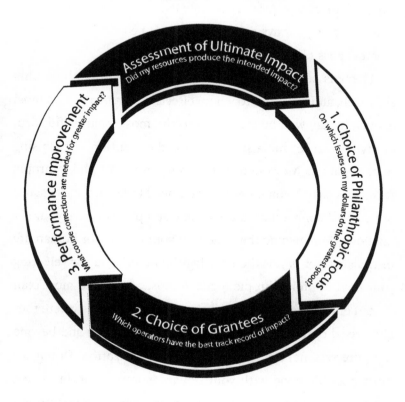

Assessment of Ultimate Impact
Did my resources produce the intended impact?

1. Choice of Philanthropic Focus
On which issues can my dollars do the greatest good?

2. Choice of Grantees
Which operators have the best track record of impact?

3. Performance Improvement
What course corrections are needed for greater impact?

1. Selection of Philanthropic Focus

Measurement matters when it comes to selecting the issues you want to focus your giving on in the first place. For example, the effective altruism movement focuses a great deal on using impact assessment data to identify the most promising issues to target from the standpoint of "doing the most good per dollar." As we've talked about in previous chapters, this is why GiveWell, Open Philanthropy, and other data hubs used by effective altruists tend to recommend giving to address neglected tropical diseases in parts of Africa and Asia. Their calculations suggest that this is one of the major ways a given dollar can be translated into the greatest possible lifesaving benefit for humanity.

There is something powerful and compelling about this approach, and for those to whom effective altruism speaks most deeply, it may well be their path to the most meaningful form of giving. But let me also offer a word of caution about using impact data as the sole driver of your choice of philanthropic focus. It's okay if you know that you need to feel a greater sense of personal connection to the people and places where your giving flows. Maximizing the benefit of your dollars for human life in the abstract is not the only legitimate criteria for selecting your field of philanthropic focus. Almost all but the most committed effective altruists select the issues and places where they give based on personally meaningful factors above and beyond the pure rational calculus of impact maximization. Doing the most possible good with your dollars is important, but when you take that utilitarian principle to the point that you no longer feel a meaningful connection to what you are doing, you run the risk of falling into the trap of spiritless giving. When this happens, the drive for objectively measurable impact can lead you into a nonrelational, untrusting, and mechanistic approach that devalues the proximity and wisdom of others. The path to meaningful giving for each of us is neither identical nor mathematically predetermined. Perhaps you are already committed to an issue or a place, regardless of whether this is the mathematically indicated way to maximize human utility. Whatever your starting point, it's worth considering what, if anything, you would have to see in the impact data to cause you to shift your philanthropic focus.

2. Selection of Funding Recipients

Second, measurement can also inform decisions about how best to allocate your giving among various organizations once you've chosen your field of focus. This is why some donors use sites like Charity Navigator. Charity Navigator has a star rating system for nonprofits based on their financial health and commitment to accountability and transparency. The idea here is that when direct measures of impact aren't readily available, these process-based indicators are a proxy for measuring how well a given organization can convert your dollars into the ultimate outcomes you are seeking as a donor. But a note of caution here: it's important to consider the nature of the problems you are trying to address with your giving before you rely on process measures as a proxy for impact. For example, just because a nonprofit advocacy organization has a high ratio of administrative expenses to program expenses on its annual 990 filing doesn't necessarily mean it's using its resources ineffectively in the complex arena of policy change.

It's also important to consider your cross-cutting commitments in this arena. Do you have preexisting relationships with certain leaders or organizations? A sense of loyalty? An extended time horizon over which you have built trust and shared perspective with grantees? Proximity to certain organizations that makes you want to stick with them regardless of whether they prove to be the highest performing based on impact measurement? Or are you focused on making one-time grants, where ongoing renewal of grantmaking is not even an issue?

3. Performance Improvement

Third, assessing impact can be an important way to help those you are funding improve their performance over time. This kind of assessment is about making course corrections while the work is underway. For instance, suppose a food bank receives funding to pilot several different outreach initiatives for recruiting volunteers to staff its distribution center. Once the data comes in, it shows that most volunteers are recruited through the "lunch and learn" talks they are giving to employees at local businesses. Now they're in a position to act on this data by doubling down on this outreach program and sunsetting their canvassing for volunteers outside the local mall.

What about your cross-cutting commitments here? Do you have a theory of change or other ideas and values that cause you to believe the work should be performed in a certain way, regardless of whether that turns out to provide the highest impact? Do you have trust and relationships that allow you to partner effectively with funding recipients to help them make use of performance data to drive improvement? Do you have additional nonfinancial capital in the form of expertise that can be useful to recipients looking to act on data to improve their operations?

DEFINING IMPACT: WHAT TYPE OF CAUSAL MECHANISM ARE YOU TRYING TO ASSESS?

Defining Impact

Maximizing your impact as a donor requires getting clear about what you actually mean by "impact." This is where the field of international economic development turns out to be pretty handy. This field has been at the forefront of impact assessment for decades, and there is a lot of helpful work to draw on. For instance, Simon Hearn and Anne Buffardi's 2016 paper "What is impact?" is a great place to start. This paper was commissioned by the Australian government as part of their efforts to better understand the impact of international economic development efforts they were funding. The authors looked across eleven different agencies involved in this field and found eleven different definitions of the term—but with many common threads.

Building on this research, here's a working definition:

Impact*: An outcome that can be causally linked back to a specific action or set of actions.*

At its heart, the idea of impact is pretty simple. First, something changes in the world—this is the "outcome." Second, we can trace that outcome back to an action or set of actions. This is how we can speak of an action having an impact. The action is connected by a causal chain to an outcome. In many cases, donors have no trouble identifying whether the outcome they are seeking is occurring or not. It proves much more difficult to figure out whether there is a causal chain linking their actions as a donor to that outcome. Let's take a closer look at this through the example of a high school tutoring program.

Impact Chain for Citywide High School Tutoring Program

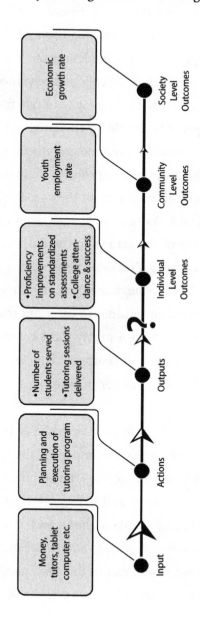

Let's say you provide funding for a local Boys and Girls Club. Your mission is to provide a comprehensive after-school tutoring program across all the public high schools in your city. By doing so, you hope to increase student proficiency on academic assessments as well as increase college attendance. You hope all this will, in turn, increase the employment rate for young people in the city, and you'd be thrilled if this program ultimately had a positive impact on the economic growth rate for the region. Even in laying this out, you can probably start to see where the challenges come in. In each step of the causal chain, the immediacy of the causal links becomes more tenuous, as shown by the decreasing size of the arrows in the illustration above. It's relatively easy to draw a direct link between the inputs into the program (which include the money you provide as a donor) and the work that the nonprofit does to carry out the program (the actions). Similarly, there's a pretty tight causal link between those actions and the program outputs in the form of the number of students served, the number of tutoring sessions delivered, and so on.

But what you really care about are the ultimate outcomes: does the program have a positive impact on the specific students it serves (individual-level outcomes) and on the broader community as a whole (community- and society-level outcomes)? Having certainty about the causal links at the far end of the chain is much more difficult. You could provide additional money to conduct a randomized, controlled trial. In this way, participation in the program would be randomly assigned to some students. Their performance on academic assessments would be compared with students in a control group who don't receive the tutoring.

Or, you could use a quasi-experimental design. In this way, program participation would not be randomly assigned. You would nevertheless attempt to estimate the program's impact by use of statistical techniques to compare participants with similar students in the general population. This might shed some light on the immediate impact of the program for participating individuals. But what about the individual impact? Does participating in the tutoring program lead to better life outcomes, such as college attendance, employment, and earnings? Trying to establish causation here would require a longer-term evaluation study, and you'd likely also encounter challenges keeping track of students over time and getting permission to access college and employment data over the years to come—and we haven't even talked about community- and society-level impacts. Here, the challenge is that you can pretty easily measure fluctuations in youth employment rates in the city and in the region's overall growth rate, but how in the world are you going to be able to tell what role the tutoring program you funded had in contributing to these changes? The causal mechanisms this far out are much more diffuse, and there are many other complicating factors outside of your control.

The same kind of challenges connecting the actions you take with the ultimate outcomes you value arise in many other fields of philanthropic endeavor. For example, accurately assessing the concept of "additionality" is vital to the integrity of carbon-offset initiatives—donors supporting these efforts must take pains to ensure they produce a reduction in greenhouse gas emissions that is "additional" to what would have taken place anyway without their intervention. This can get so involved that some of the entities responsible for verifying carbon offsets have over two hundred project-specific protocols and methodologies.[19]

In case all this starts to feel overwhelming, it's important to bear in mind that for the great majority of donors, meaningfully assessing the impact of your giving doesn't have to become an intimidating obstacle. This is where it's helpful to turn to the work of Alnoor Ebrahim and his 2019 book, *Measuring Social Change*. As he points out, there are really just two big factors we need to track when we are seeking to evaluate impact. The first is the certainty of the links in the causal chain, and second is the degree of control that any given actor has over the ultimate outcome at the end of the causal chain.

1. How Certain Are the Causal Links in Your Impact Chain?

It can be helpful to note the distinction between causal chains that are simple, those that are complicated, and those that are complex. Remember the definitions of these three kinds of challenges from Chapter 4. In a simple causal chain, one action is directly linked to another, and the results are easily replicable time after time. An oft-cited example for this is the recipe for baking chocolate chip cookies.[20] If you follow the steps the same way each time, you will get the same result. A "complicated" causal chain is linear, just like a simple one; it just has a lot more steps. For example, launching a satellite into orbit takes many more steps than baking cookies, but the process is predictable and replicable. It does, however, require tremendous attention to detail and technical expertise, since a deviation at any one of the multiple steps in the causal chain can lead to a dramatically different result.

A complex causal chain is another order of business entirely. A classic example is the process of parenting a child. Even if you try to raise two children in exactly the same way, you won't get the same result—there are way too many contingent factors.

2. How Much Control Do You Have over the Outcomes You Ultimately Care About?

There's no guarantee that the outcomes you care about are actually within your or your associates' span of control. It can be helpful here to think in terms of three spheres of influence.[21]

First, there is your sphere of control. This is where you can produce outcomes directly through your own actions. Attribution of impact is unquestioned. For example, you were the sole donor to the capital campaign that paid for the construction of a new soup kitchen.

Second, there is your sphere of direct influence. This is where you can observe others producing outcomes as a directly traceable result of your actions. Attribution of impact is linear and direct. For example, you gave money to expand a high school tutoring program to a new school. In a randomized trial, you learn the students participating in that program had an average increase of twenty points on their reading proficiency versus the control group.

Finally, there is your sphere of indirect influence. This is where you can observe others producing outcomes that are in some way traceable back to your actions. Impact is best understood in terms of *contribution* rather than *attribution*. The chain of causation is nonlinear and involves multiple parties. For example, you gave money to an advocacy organization that worked in a coalition with five other groups. The coalition lobbied successfully to pass legislation that provides public funding for expanding that high school tutoring program statewide. Five years after implementation of this state-funded program, college attendance rates are up 6 percent statewide. Did your money—which enabled the advocacy campaign—contribute to this positive outcome? Probably, but it almost certainly wasn't the only factor resulting in the ultimate outcome of higher college attendance.

ATTRIBUTION VS. CONTRIBUTION: WHAT KIND OF IMPACT APPETITE DO YOU HAVE?

Here's why these two questions about causal chains and spheres of influence might matter a lot to your giving. In a perfect world, we'd all like to have high impact outcomes that are directly attributable to our giving. However, if you are interested in addressing complex challenges like intergenerational poverty, chronic homelessness, and disparities in educational attainment, it may be very difficult to establish a clear causal link between the actions you take and the ultimate outcomes you are seeking. The causal links themselves aren't certain, and the ultimate outcomes you value are outside your and your grantees' direct control and/or direct influence.

This is why it is so important to keep in mind the distinction between attribution and contribution. It's natural to want to be able to directly attribute impact to your giving: *my* dollars produced *this* change in the world. But if that is what you insist on, you will be limited to giving on issues where you have direct control or direct influence over outcomes. This leaves out many of the complex social challenges that are most in need of your support. If you are willing to accept contribution when it comes to assessing the impact of your giving, you have many more options for meaningful giving. Indeed, many of the savviest donors have discovered that they can make a much larger contribution to the world through indirect influence than they can through direct action or direct influence. So, beware of the temptation to insist on attributing impact outside the sphere of your direct influence. Remember that story we started the chapter with. If you insist that your grantees tell you about how your specific dollars made the critical difference, chances are they'll only be making things up, and you'll be fooling yourself. Along the way, you'll also be distorting the work of your grantees and falling into the trap of selfish giving!

Here's a question for further reflection: if you had to choose between making an indirect contribution to a globally significant outcome and helping a single person in a small way that you knew was directly attributable to your own efforts, which would you prefer? While it may provide valuable insight to consider this question in such stark terms, the trade-offs between the level of social impact and direct attribution in your giving are not always so extreme. This is illustrated as a scatter plot with (x,y) coordinates on the figure below. The vertical axis represents the level of social impact achieved, and the horizontal axis represents the degree to which you can directly attribute that ultimate impact to your own giving. Your impact comfort zone is the area of this plot where you can find satisfaction as a donor.

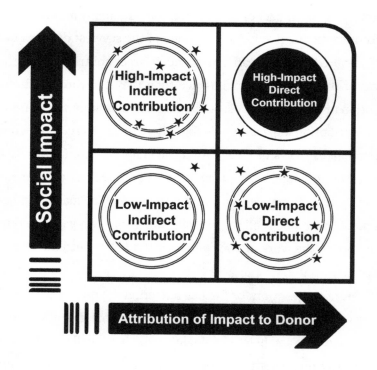

Almost all donors would prefer to land in the upper-right quadrant and stay out of the lower-left quadrant. How much other territory are you comfortable with? For example, can you wrap your head around long-term funding for an advocacy organization that is working in coalition with many others to ultimately enact a sweeping policy change? Let's say the issue is about rewriting the rules for agricultural subsidies in a way that will better address the threats of climate change and food insecurity. When that policy is finally changed, the social impact will be profound, but you will have to be comfortable knowing that your grantmaking indirectly contributed to this outcome. You won't be able to attribute the outcome directly to your own giving. On the flip side, would you rather give your resources to a local food bank, where you can directly count the number of additional people fed with every check you write? In this case, you can feel very certain that your specific dollars are making a concrete difference for people, but you will also have to settle for achieving less impact at a systemic level.

Whatever your ideal preferences, the most important thing is to get clarity about what range of impact attribution is acceptable to you as a donor. The next step is to consider whether you can develop your own psychological flexibility to expand that range. The more you can cultivate your appetite for indirect contribution, the greater your possibilities for maximizing the overall impact of your giving, even if you can't directly attribute it to yourself. It really does make a difference in your giving if you are willing to stretch and grow your own psychology as a philanthropist.

Conclusion: Key Takeaways On Assessing the Impact of Your Giving

- Metrics and milestones are most useful when the causal chain is simple and outcomes are easily controlled by actors. They risk being a distraction and a distortion of grantee activities when you insist on using them on organizations engaged in complex, adaptive strategies.

- "Intelligence analysis" is the best approach when dealing with complexity and long causal chains.[22] The more complex the causal chain and the more indirect the actor's influence over outcomes, the more proximity, patience, and trust you need to truly assess impact.

- Positive intentions are not enough to guarantee positive impact—proximity, flexibility, and trust go a long way to making course corrections.

- Don't let fixation on attribution trump your opportunity to make a contribution. As a donor, remember you have a special role to play in making this possible by not requiring grantees to compete for claiming impact, especially when the work itself requires ongoing collaboration.

- You don't actually have to measure impact or be able to precisely define the impact of your giving to have an impact. What you know about your giving's impact and the actual impact of your giving are two separate things.

In conclusion, it's worth remembering that honoring the four commitments of meaningful giving can be really helpful when it comes to your approach to measuring impact. This is particularly true of the commitment to *get real*—seek and speak the truth to everyone, including yourself—and the commitment to *get together*—treat others with consideration, not contempt. Now, it's time to delve even more deeply into the commitment to get together, beginning with a closer look at how you build your team when it comes to getting help with gearing up your giving.

9

GETTING TOGETHER

Constructing Your Team

---

*"The best way to find out if you can trust
somebody is to trust them."*

—ERNEST HEMINGWAY

Many donors looking to take their giving to the next level get stuck
on the question of how to bring on the staff they need. There are
no hard and fast rules in this area, and donors have answered this
question across an entire spectrum. At one end is the Bill and
Melinda Gates Foundation. It has nearly 2,000 employees and
spends several billion dollars in annual grantmaking. At the other
end, the large majority of family foundations in the US have no
paid staff at all, even though some of these unstaffed foundations
give away tens of millions of dollars each year.

This is why the first thing to figure out is whether you need to bring on a team at all. To get started, let's go back to the "Who" exercises we worked on in Chapter 3's Ten W's. There, we looked at six options for DIY giving:

- Go simple and straightforward
- Go blue chip
- Go boutique
- Go passive
- Go with your gut
- Go pro

If one or more of these approaches feels like a fit for you, then by all means don't staff up! But what if none of those options sets you up for giving that truly makes sense? What if you really do need to get some help? This is where it's time to return to another key exercise from Chapter 3. Remember the "Who" section, about making two maps of the decision-making roles and responsibilities in your giving? The first of these charts lists who is making the decisions in your giving currently. The second maps out what your ideal decision-making configuration is moving forward. If your first chart and your second chart are pretty much the same and you're already feeling impactful and fulfilled with your giving, perhaps this chapter won't have as much to offer you. That would indicate the team you currently have is already meeting your needs. However, if you have some work to do fielding a team, it's time to read on!

STAFFING UP:
FOUR KINDS OF HELP FOR DONORS

Let's start by looking at the different options you have when it comes to getting help. I've found it's helpful to think in terms of four different kinds of help as you gear up your giving. In this section, we'll walk through each of these options and assist you in thinking about what might be the best fit for you.

Hired Help: They follow your direct instructions to paint inside the lines under your ongoing supervision. These are people who show up as having an E for execute on your decision-making chart from Chapter 3. On that chart, hired help mostly shows up in the column for routine managerial and administrative tasks. Think of administrative staff tasked to support the distribution of funds from your family foundation as part of their broader duties within your family office.

Faithful Steward: These people protect your interests while carrying out your decisions. They make sure the paint stays inside the lines you have designated while your attention is elsewhere. These are people who show up on your decision-making chart with an E (execute) and also an I (inform). This means you need to inform your steward about decisions after the fact so they can effectively represent and advance your interests while you are away. Occasionally, you may also ask people in this role to have a P, where they are proposing specific actions for your consideration. This is most likely to happen in the routine managerial tasks column.

A faithful steward might also have a C, in that on some issues you consult with them prior to making the decision. Often, this is to get their views on whether the course of action you intend can be executed effectively under their oversight. Take, for example, how you might interact with a wealth advisor or senior client manager from a private bank. They will make sure your book-keeper and accountant are on the same page with your estate attorney. However, don't confuse a faithful steward with a true, trusted advisor. A faithful steward's role stops at helping you implement the decisions you've made on your own. They are not there to point out your blind spots or otherwise save you from yourself.

Trusted Advisor: This is someone who focuses on what to get done and why, including advising you to paint outside the lines of your own comfort zone when they judge that would actually be the best way to advance both the social impact you are seeking as well as your own growth and personal fulfillment. A key way that trusted advisors are different from faithful stewards and hired help is that they have significant responsibility to propose courses of action to you (P) in a number of columns on the chart. They might advise on everything from overall strategy to governance decisions to resource allocation for social impact and market return. Trusted advisors might also play a role in executing (E) decisions once they are made, but they stop short of making major decisions. That is still your role. They might also have C's and I's in your decision-making chart if you consult them before making certain decisions or inform them after the fact.

Delegated Decision-Maker: This is someone with whom you have entrusted full decision-making authority over a defined area of your affairs. They decide what to do and how to do it, and they ensure it gets done. These are people who show up as having D's on your chart, sometimes just in one column, such as resource allocation decisions for social impact, and sometimes across all the columns. An example would be when you fully outsource the management of your financial affairs to an independent money manager. In this case, you are giving them full authority over the allocation of your funds across a range of investments. When you work with a delegated decision-maker, you may hold onto the C, meaning you must be consulted before certain kinds of decisions are made. Or, you may simply have an I, meaning they have an obligation to inform you of a decision they have made after the fact.

How do you decide which kind of help is the best fit for you? Consider what role you honestly want to play in the decisions around your giving. If you want to retain the final say on all matters and you are prepared to stay involved overseeing day-to-day operations, then hired help may be all you need. That would be a fine solution if you just want an extra set of hands to help carry out routine tasks that are easily delegated. On the other hand, if you'd like to be able to step away from day-to-day oversight and have confidence that your directions are being well executed, then a faithful steward might be best. If you're not sure what to do or how to maximize your impact and fulfillment but still want to make the final decisions, then you might consider a trusted advisor. If you want to step back much more and truly farm out your giving lock, stock, and barrel, then a delegated decision-maker may be best for you.

MATCHING YOUR TEAM TO THE LEVEL OF CHALLENGE

Your choice about what kind of help to secure should also be connected to the nature of the problems you are trying to address. This is where it's helpful to recall the distinction we looked at in Chapter 8 between simple, complicated, and complex problems. It's important to match the type of help you bring on with the level of problem you are going after. Unless you are prepared to go pro and devote a truly substantial portion of your time to your giving, there are certain minimum requirements for what type of help you need to be successful at each level of challenge.

Hired Help Usually Suffices for Simple Challenges

When you are engaged with a simple challenge, you can reliably produce the desired outcome by following a straightforward process. In this case, it's not hard to convert your financial resources into a positive impact for other people. This means that with simple problems, it's pretty easy to succeed on a DIY basis or with hired help if you'd like to save some of your own time. For example, it's not hard to find a local food pantry to which you can donate resources. Those resources translate directly into feeding hungry people.

Faithful Stewards Work Well to Oversee Complicated Challenges

With complicated challenges, there are many steps and players in the causal chain. Still, producing impact here is a fairly linear process—you simply may need more help to keep track of it all. A faithful steward who can devote the time and attention to the multiple elements in the causal chain may be particularly helpful in this situation. Somebody has to make sure the different steps are effectively connected and integrated because if the chain doesn't link up or if it breaks at any point, you lose impact. If a single component is faulty, the satellite doesn't make it into orbit.

This is also where someone with practical proximity can really come in handy. They can more easily connect the pieces effectively, and they have technical knowledge informing them about what is needed to make effective linkages between different parts of the chain. For example, let's say you want to help get a supportive housing program going in your city. Suppose this involves a three-way partnership with a housing authority, a social service agency that provides case management services, and a local hospital system. It's a huge asset to have someone on your team who has worked on the ground in one or more of these agencies; this kind of person deeply understands how the pieces best fit together and can quickly improvise a patch in case of breakdown.

Seek Out Trusted Advisors or Delegated Decision-Makers When You Take On Complex Challenges

Complex, emergent challenges are an entirely different order of business. For example, let's say you want to change public policy to establish a new civil right for children to access high-quality public education. There are a lot of options for how you might go about this, from backing a ballot initiative campaign that would amend your state's constitution to supporting a broad coalition of advocacy organizations to lobby lawmakers. The path to achieving this outcome is not linear. Your strategy cannot be fully laid out in advance—it involves the need to adjust on the fly to emergent circumstances that no one can fully predict. This is why having people on your team with practical proximity to the system and its dynamics is so important, particularly when the object of your giving is to change a complex, dynamic system. Practical proximity to a system is associated with pattern recognition and a degree of predictive power in a highly uncertain context. So, unless you bring those qualities yourself, it's likely you'll need a trusted advisor or a delegated decision-maker on your team when you want to tackle complex challenges.

Build Your Team to Complement Your Own Level of Passion, Proximity, and Perspective

If you are strongly drawn to focus your giving on complex challenges, it makes sense to look more deeply at what it takes to put together a winning team. This kind of giving is by far the most demanding of you and your team. It takes certain personal qualities to do this well:

1. Sustained passion for social contribution on complex challenges
2. Practical proximity to the issue at hand
3. Elevated psychological perspective, which has two key dimensions:
   - Self-development: Your level of self-awareness and care for yourself (how invested are you in your own journey of growth and development?)
   - Self-transcendence: Your level of awareness and care for others (to what extent can you focus on meeting the needs of others ahead of your own?)

Determining where you are regarding these three qualities is an important first step. This informs who will best complement you as you build out your team. There are three questions you can ask yourself to figure out where you come out:

1. Do you expect to have sustained passion for solving complex social challenges in a given arena? Is your commitment to the issue you're focused on high and durable? For example, how well do these prompts describe you:
   - I stick with my interests for a long period of time.
   - I know this issue well and have been working on it for years already.
   - I handle frustration and setbacks by staying committed.

2. Do you have practical proximity to the issue you've chosen to focus on, such that your pattern recognition and predictive power about the system's dynamics gives you a reliable understanding about what to do to maximize impact as circumstances shift over time? For example, how much does this sound like you:

   - I've been personally impacted by this issue in a significant way—I know why it's a problem in personal terms.
   - I have family members and/or friends who are currently impacted by this issue.
   - I've been involved in day-to-day operations for an organization that works on addressing the root causes of this issue.

3. Do you have a highly developed level of awareness and care for yourself as well as others? For example:

   - I am generally aware of my typical patterns of thoughts, feelings, and actions and how they impact my state of mind in any given moment.
   - I have well-developed routines of self-care that I practice on a daily basis.
   - I have a clear understanding of what makes me feel the most meaning and fulfillment, and I have oriented my life to move toward those things.
   - I seek to show up as a resourceful, positive presence for those around me.
   - Friends, colleagues, and family find me approachable and are comfortable being vulnerable with me.

So, if you want to take on the most complex social challenges with your giving, the upshot is pretty simple.

If you don't already have a highly developed level of awareness and care for yourself and others, you should consider working with a coach to help you become your best self and find fulfillment in your giving. If you don't have practical proximity to the issues you want to focus on, there's value in seeking that by proxy through a trusted advisor who proposes strategy and investments or a delegated decision-maker who makes these decisions on your behalf. Finally, if you don't have a sustained passion for navigating the complexity of the social challenges you are tackling, you should consider delegating decision-making to someone who brings not only that passion but also the wisdom and pattern recognition that come with practical proximity to the issues at hand.

When you combine these three factors, you get the following guide to building your team:

You Have: Sustained Passion for Systems Change	You Have: Practical Proximity to the System You're Trying to Change	You Have: Highly Developed Awareness and Care for Yourself and Others	What You Need in Your Team
✓	✓	✓	DIY (with hired help or faithful steward as desired)
✓	✓	✗	DIY with trusted advisor as coach (and hired help or faithful steward as desired)
✓	✗	✗	Trusted advisor with practical proximity + coaching
✓	✗	✓	Trusted advisor with practical proximity
✗	✗	✗	Delegated decision maker in collaboration with trusted advisor as coach
✗	✗	✓	Delegated decision maker
✗	✓	✗	Delegated decision maker in collaboration with trusted advisor as coach
✗	✓	✓	Delegated decision maker (or trusted advisor if you prefer to be a bit more actively engaged)

SOURCING YOUR TEAM

Even after you've figured out what kind of help you need, finding the right people to fill those roles often feels like a significant barrier. How do you source great people for these different levels of help?

Sourcing Hired Help

Finding hired help offers the lowest stakes. They are going to be operating under continuous supervision, whether yours or that of a faithful steward. They might need to have certain technical expertise, but generally speaking, you don't need any special sourcing to make these hires. Even so, it can be helpful to have a system for sourcing talent at all levels: Geoffrey Smart's *Who: The A-Method for Hiring* is a great resource to draw on as you develop your "people process."

Sourcing Faithful Stewards

Faithful stewards are often sourced by starting out with someone you already trust, whom you've then asked to help with your giving. One pattern I've seen a lot is that donors have someone in a family office or business, or they simply have a longtime friend with whom they've built a high-trust, working relationship over a period of years. These people are often asked to take on more and more responsibility with a donor to help them carry out their giving. Faithful stewards with no particular expertise or connection to the issues your giving is focused on can quickly get in over their heads. This is particularly true if it turns out that the problems at hand are actually complex, dynamic systems, not subject to straightforward causal-chain approaches. As the saying goes, "You don't know what you don't know."

Sourcing Trusted Advisors

What about trusted advisors? Where do you go to find someone for this kind of role? Bringing on a trusted advisor requires significant willingness to stretch and grow on the part of the donor. That said, the benefits are commensurate with the challenge. Great, effective trusted advisors in philanthropy are people who are able to embrace a donor's perspective and interests while also authentically leveraging their own passion, practical experience, and proximity. This is how trusted advisors help the donor achieve both lasting social impact and personal fulfillment—and even joy!

In the relationship between an advisor and a donor, mutual trust is crucial. Seeking and speaking the truth about the complexities of making change is vital to unlocking high-impact philanthropy. When there is mutual trust, the donor is able to fully share not just their goals for social impact but also what they are truly seeking in terms of meaning and fulfillment. Likewise, the advisor is able to share their full and honest perspective, even when this is challenging for the donor to hear.

Unfortunately, dysfunctional relationships between advisors and donors are all too common. In many cases, the advisors whom donors engage to help with their giving—whether family foundation staff or consultants on contract—fear that the relationship with the donor won't survive sustained truth-telling. They sense that what the donor really wants is a faithful steward, or even simply hired help, rather than a true trusted advisor.

When a donor does take the leap to seek out a trusted advisor, the biggest mistake they typically make is that they start with trust and try to build proximity and passion. In effect, they try to grow a faithful steward into a trusted advisor. This is actually much harder than taking the opposite approach.

My advice is to seek out the people who have a proven passion for a subject, practical experience with the systems surrounding that issue, and proximity to the people you seek to impact. When you identify those people, you can then work to build trusting relationships with them. It's usually far easier than you might think.

How do you find those people? Here are two approaches you can take:

1. Look for philanthropic advisors who have a background in social entrepreneurship. Advisors who have come from the ranks of social entrepreneurs often have deep, practical experience. They typically continue to maintain close connections to the issues and the networks within which they previously worked directly. So, when you're evaluating potential advisors, don't substitute "expertise" and polish around concepts and ideas for practical experience and proximity.

2. Be open to building trusted advising relationships with active leaders of social enterprises. This might seem

counterintuitive. How can someone who is actively raising money for their own change-making venture not have a conflict of interest providing trusted advice to you? But the evidence is right there. These are folks who have chosen time and again over the course of their lives to give their all to tackling some of society's toughest challenges. In far more instances than you might think, you can trust these committed change agents to prioritize impact—even if that means setting aside their own ask—to help you make the best possible allocation of resources. They usually do not shy away from opportunities to address the very challenges they have dedicated their lives to solving.

Sourcing Delegated Decision-Makers

What about finding a delegated decision-maker? Where do you go to find people to fill this kind of role? One great opportunity is to look for pooled social-impact funds that are run by social entrepreneurs who are both passionate and proximate to the issues you want to address. Recently, more and more social entrepreneurs have been coming together to create philanthropic funds to attract investment and provide direct advice to funders about how to allocate resources. For example, look at the Black Voices for Black Justice Fund, the Southern Reconstruction Fund, and The 1954 Project. In these funds, a whole array of Black social entrepreneurs with lifelong commitments to key issues are joining together to amplify the voices of other Black social entrepreneurs.

Together, they work to build power across all kinds of issues and communities. These funds allow those with a lot of wisdom and proximity to particular issues to focus philanthropists' attention on compelling change agents whose work is already making a meaningful impact on those issues.

Another option for finding delegated decision-makers is to start with a trusted advisor who is already part of your team. Simply give them greater responsibility for making decisions on your behalf. The very attributes of passion, proximity, and psychological maturity that make people great trusted advisors can also make them great delegated decision-makers.

10

WORKING
EFFECTIVELY
WITH OTHERS

Treat Others with Consideration,
Not Contempt

The human project is to remain human
and to block the dehumanization
and estrangement of others."

—TONI MORRISON

Imagine a philanthropist who loves to support the arts and gives a large grant of general operating support to a community-based music organization. So far, so good. Now, imagine it's six months later and the executive director is planning the organization's annual gala. The philanthropist's lead staffer calls to say, "We really need you to create space in the program at your gala for my boss to speak about a wonderful new public art installation that we're trying to get planning permission for in a neighboring town." This might seem like an innocuous request, but how much choice does the executive director really feel they have in this situation? The donor might become offended if the executive director doesn't immediately accept—*don't they remember how much money we give them every year?*

So, was this grant truly a gift or a calculated transaction that came at a price?

Chances are, if you are committed to doing your philanthropy differently and better, there's much in this story that turns you off. Unfortunately, this kind of thing happens all the time in philanthropy. Sometimes, it even occurs in subtle ways where the donors involved don't even realize how their actions are negatively impacting others.

There's a straightforward framework for giving differently. It starts with the following commitment of meaningful giving: treat others with consideration, not contempt. This is about fully appreciating other people's perspective and agency as you seek to make the world a better place through your giving.

So, as a donor how do you follow through on this commitment to treat others with consideration, not contempt? The reality is that meaningful giving comes about through dynamic relationships with others. How you show up with other people is crucial to your impact and joy as a donor. We'll start with a conceptual framework for understanding the range of possibilities for how we relate to others. We'll look at six principles for applying this framework in our relationships with others. Then, we'll explore five hands-on tools that you can use to build your skills for communicating more effectively with others in challenging situations. The best part is that these tools and the skills you get from putting them into practice are useful not just for creating more joy and more impact in your giving but in all the areas of your life.

A CONCEPTUAL FRAMEWORK:
THE SPECTRUM OF
INTERPERSONAL DYNAMICS

Stepping up our effectiveness working with other people starts with recognizing the full spectrum of ways that human beings relate to each other. The graphic that follows might look complex, but the core idea is pretty simple. The closer we are to the middle of this spectrum, the more collaborative we are with each other—and the more the solutions we devise are co-created, the more lasting these solutions are. If your goal is to use your philanthropic resources to create meaningful change that outlasts your own giving, working to develop solutions to which all parties are truly committed is important. Co-created solutions are inherently more sustainable than those that require continued persuasion or even coercion to maintain. Indeed, how you engage with others often holds the key to shifting entrenched systems with relatively limited philanthropic resources.

The Spectrum of Interpersonal Dynamics

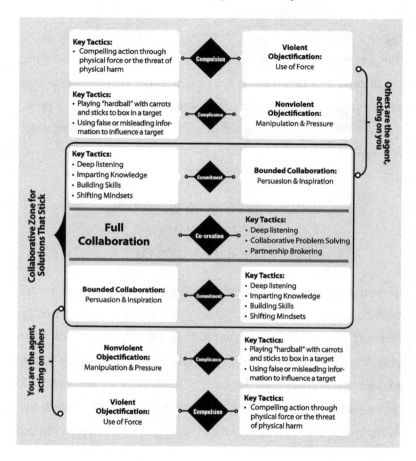

SIX PRINCIPLES FOR
WORKING EFFECTIVELY WITH OTHERS

1. Start with deep listening. Be genuinely curious to understand what is important to the other person. What feelings and experiences do they value the most? What are

their rules for experiencing these feelings? What are the most pressing challenges they experience? What is their vision for making the world a better place? What ideas do they have about solving the problems they care about?

2. After careful listening and thoughtful evaluation, look for opportunities to engage in full collaboration. This is about co-creating a course of action with the other person such that you both have ownership over the game plan.

2. Be genuinely open to being persuaded by another's understanding of the problem and their plans for solving it.

4. If you can't find a fully collaborative solution, only now do you engage in persuasion and inspiration where you seek to move the other person to commit to the course of action you believe is best.

5. As a last resort, if the other party is still unmoved to take action by rational persuasion and inspiration, you could consider using pressure tactics. Understand that you may get a short-term win this way, but the best you can hope for when you use this form of influence is compliance. *This is rarely the way to create solutions that truly endure.*

6. Don't use violence except in self-defense to counter violence.

Now, let's explore each of these principles in more detail.

1. Begin with Deep Listening

Did you know that 67 percent of American men would rather administer a mild electric shock to themselves than sit quietly with their own thoughts for as little as six minutes? That's pretty crazy, but it's true. This was the finding from a series of experiments done at University of Virginia and published in *Science Magazine* in July 2014. And, by the way, 25 percent of women also took the shocking way out. Unfortunately, it seems pretty clear that many of us are not comfortable with deep listening—even when it comes to listening to ourselves.

Anytime you want to engage with someone on a truly practical basis to solve problems in a lasting way, start with deep listening. Seek an understanding of what someone else is most interested in, what problems they see, and what solutions, if any, they are focused on pursuing. What do they think needs to be done to make the world a better place? How do they currently go about meeting their common human needs? What vehicles are they most reliant on for meeting those needs? What are the roots of their joy? What are the triggers for their fear and anger?

Deep listening has several key attributes. It is:

- Rooted in genuine curiosity
- Seeks understanding
- Steps outside your own psychology
- Opens you up to being moved
- Asks nothing in return—it is a gift, not a transaction

Deep listening matters so much because it speaks to one of the human heart's deepest desires: to be fully appreciated for who we really are. And it is rare. In her book *You're Not Listening*, journalist Kate Murphy recounts that she was moved to write the book by the realization that humanity is losing the art of listening. As she puts it, "To listen well is to figure out what's on someone's mind and demonstrate that you care enough to want to know. It's what we all crave; to be understood as a person with thoughts, emotions, and intentions that are unique and valuable and deserving of attention."

Why are so many of us falling down when it comes to summoning our faculties and really listening for understanding and deep connection with others? The simple answer is that it is hard. One reason is physiological. Perhaps this is God's joke on us, but human beings are built to speak at about 125 words per minute while our brains are built to process language at up to 800 words per minute. That's a whole lot of spare processing power while you're on the listening side of a conversation. You might think that would make it easier to listen deeply, but it's just the opposite. All the extra processing power means we can go in all kinds of distracting directions, like listening to our inner voice while still following the gist of what someone else is saying. Deep listening requires an affirmative choice to devote our higher-level faculties fully to the task of understanding what someone else is saying in the face of continuous mental distraction.

Deep listening requires knowledge about what deep listening is and why it matters. It also requires discipline, a bit like practicing meditation, where whenever your mind starts to wander, you gently bring yourself back into the moment. It requires a mindset too. You need to value deep listening such that you want to connect and understand others despite the difficulty.

I have found that all three of these—knowledge, skills, and mindset—need to be stacked together to be most effective. What makes the other person tick? How can I understand their motivations and mental processes as fully as possible? Remember the model of human psychology grounded in seven universal human needs? Listen for meaning and insight with this framework in mind.

As you listen, get curious about how the other person meets their innate, egocentric drives for security, novelty, social status, and social connection. How do they satisfy their higher-level needs for social contribution and personal growth? How do they tie together these universal human drives with their particular thoughts, feelings, and, ultimately, actions? Even though we all have the same core set of psychological needs, there are an infinite variety of ways that individuals go about meeting these needs. This is just one of the reasons people are endlessly fascinating and worthy of your deep listening.

2. Try for Full Collaboration and Collaborative Problem-Solving

Building on the foundation of deep listening, your next step is to share from your own heart if there's any kind of an opening to do so. Push yourself to go outside your comfort zone in this sharing process. This is an important point because your instincts are often going to tell you to do the opposite, to seek advantage by holding your cards close to the vest.

I'm here to tell you this is an inferior, old-school methodology for working with other people. When you share from the heart, you begin to build a powerful basis of shared context and understanding. You don't have to bare your soul. Even being frank about what your own bottom-line interests are in a given situation can open up incredible opportunities for win-win, collaborative problem-solving. True understanding of each other's key issues and interests is a powerful place from which to identify common problems and the potential for working together to develop solutions that really stick.

Consider the classic case taught in Harvard's Program on Negotiation in which two parties are tasked with negotiating who gets a single orange. One of them wants to make orange juice, and the other wants to use the rind to bake some cookies. Without sharing their goals with each other, they won't discover the win-win solution that is right in front of them.

Finding these win-win outcomes is the basis for a technique called "collaborative problem-solving." It's actually something that works great with children; my wife and I have not looked back since we found this approach in a book called *Raising Human Beings* by Ross Greene. You can also apply this approach to almost any situation in the adult world when you need to get concerns on the table and find a solution that everyone can agree on. Here's the structured format:

- You begin by asking the other person to identify all their concerns.
- You repeat them back for understanding.
- You check for more, ensuring you've got all their concerns out on the table.
- You share your own concerns.
- You do not comment on each other's concerns or argue about them. Concerns constitute subjective feelings, which aren't open for debate—they're not empirically right or wrong.
- The two of you look creatively at the whole pile of concerns and see what you can come up with that you can agree on as a satisfactory way to meet everyone's concerns.

This might sound too simple to work, but it is surprisingly effective in the real world, from navigating nap time with a preschooler to hashing out the terms of a funding agreement with a grantee. As you try this technique, you may find that the hardest part is listening attentively to the other person's concerns without jumping in with your position and concerns of your own. It's particularly helpful to use this technique with someone you need to work with repeatedly. Over time, you both come to trust the process, recognizing that more often than not, you can come up with something that addresses both of your most important concerns. Perhaps the most important benefit is that when you solve problems this way, you end up with solutions that are co-created.

This makes these solutions much more likely to be implemented and honored by all parties concerned. When you solve problems this way, they have a much greater chance of staying solved!

3. Be Genuinely Open to Being Persuaded by Another's Ideas

Failing to be genuinely open to another's ideas is where a lot of philanthropy goes wrong. Selfish and spiritless giving often take place because the donor is so deeply attached to their own plan. They know what action they want others to take, and the name of the game in their giving is all about getting the other parties to play their assigned roles. You are opening yourself up to all kinds of unanticipated consequences and negative feedback loops if you operate like this. Unfortunately, this is exactly how so much philanthropy takes place.

There are several classic cognitive biases that come into play when you approach the world this way: confirmation bias, recency bias, reactance bias, anchoring, the fundamental attribution error—the list goes on. Working in a silo and trying to enlist other people in your predetermined plan is not the path for meaningful giving. It's not how you develop solutions that stick in a complex world where the other people have independent access to their own information and options. The most pressing problems you really care about solving *would already be solved* if it were this easy to command and control your way to the solution.

It could very well be that the other party has a perspective on the problem that you have missed. This doesn't mean blindly following someone else's lead simply because they ask you to. Coming from a place of openness and trust doesn't require you to suspend your critical-thinking faculties. You need to evaluate their point of view and test whether it might plausibly be a better way to achieve a shared objective than whatever you initially had in mind.

This is why the first several steps of working effectively with others are grounded in opening yourself up to the other person's perspective. You start with deep listening. You share your own wants, needs, and interests. You engage in collaborative problem-solving, where you look for creative ways to satisfy both of your interests. You also make yourself open to being positively influenced by the other party. You don't assume you have a monopoly on the truth or the right course of action. You open yourself up to rational persuasion and inspiration. You think critically about what actions make the most sense in light of the interests that you and your counterparty just shared.

4. When You Have To, Use Rational Persuasion and Inspiration

There are still going to be times when you need to engage in rational persuasion and inspiration to positively influence others. When you have a clear idea about what action needs to be taken next, sometimes you need to influence the other party to take that action. Remember the four key functional roles for advancing social change we talked about in Chapter 4? Entrepreneurs are often in the role of seeking to persuade and inspire others to join with them in pursuing a specific course of action. Think about Dustin Moskowitz and Cari Tuna and the role they are playing seeking to build a movement of effective altruism among fellow philanthropists.

This is where we begin to move below the line of pure collaboration into what you might call "bounded collaboration." To be less fancy, you could just call this rational persuasion and inspiration. So, what are the tools and techniques you need to put into play here? This is where it's helpful to remember the following model:

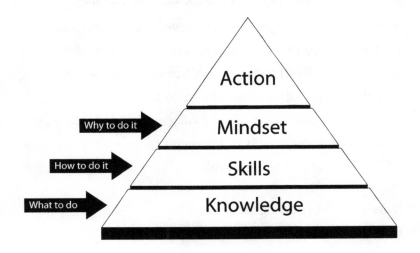

Helping move people to action is about helping them get past each of these gateways by imparting knowledge, building skills, and shifting mindsets.

Let's talk about each of these modes of influence and how to show up in the best possible way in each arena. The first thing is to figure out what the other person's barriers to action might be. You have in mind a solution to a problem, and the solution requires this other person to take a certain action or set of actions. Begin by asking yourself why they haven't already acted in this way. Is it a lack of knowledge, meaning they simply don't know what action to take? Is it a lack of skill, meaning they don't know *how* to take action? Or is it an issue of mindset? Perhaps they don't want to take this particular action because they don't see it as being aligned with their own beliefs and interests.

Imparting Knowledge: Increasing the Value of Learning

When it comes to imparting knowledge, it is important to focus on what is going to make the person care about the information. Why will knowing this piece of information provide something that the person values? One way to do this is to increase their sense of the ongoing cost of not paying attention to this. So, you want to paint the benefit of learning this knowledge but also underscore the cost of not learning it.

Building Skills: Creating the Context for Continuous Practice

When it comes to helping people acquire skills, you want to create the context in which the person can do repetitions for mastery. This is why so many self-taught chefs who opened their own restaurants have excelled. You get a whole lot more practice when the customer is paying for the ingredients as opposed to a culinary school in which your tuition must pay for it all.

Shifting Mindset: Showing Up as a Coach to Support Self-Discovery

When it comes to trying to shift mindset, it's worth remembering that people must own their own transformation. Very rarely can you simply tell someone what perspective they've been missing and have them change their mind. Still, people do hate to be internally inconsistent. This means they need to move through a progression of shifting beliefs to fully change their own perspective on a given issue. One of the most effective things you can do to help is engage in a coaching mode, where you are asking questions and encouraging people to challenge themselves and open up to a higher and better version of themselves. As a coach, the core of what you are doing is supporting someone's process of self-discovery. You want to help them reach realizations like:

- This is possible for me.
- I have already achieved or operated at this higher level in some other area of my life.
- I don't have to do this alone. I can draw support from key people, places, and things around me to support my own evolution.
- I am excited to take this on, and rising to this challenge is how I roll. I can align with my highest and best self by honoring the challenge of changing perspective.
- I can rewrite my mental rules to make this possible.

Great coaching is about encouraging people to make clear their highest values as well as their established patterns of behavior, motivating them to close the gap between how they show up moment to moment and who they are capable of being. What feelings do they most want to have? What are their rules for experiencing those feelings? What has to happen for them to feel that way? Remind them that they made up these rules in the first place to serve a purpose, and if the rules are no longer serving them, they can change them.

In a great many cases, once people open up their perspective and shift their mindset, they find that the necessary knowledge and skills are right there already. They already know what to do and how to do it, so they can jump right into action.

5. Pressure Tactics Are a Last Resort— They Rarely Lead to Stable, Sustainable Solutions

When you have total clarity about a course of action you need others to take in pursuit of the greater good *yet* they have remained resistant to your attempts to use persuasion and inspiration, you may want to play hardball. Even so, you should remember there is often a cost to doing so. You may experience a short-term victory if you use these tactics successfully, but the end result is often less durable because the other party is not committed to it—they are merely compliant.

What do pressure tactics actually look like? Classic advocacy involves boxing your target in and leaving them only one way to go: the way you want them to. An example of this would be threatening to mount a primary challenge to an elected official because they haven't supported your policy priorities on a clean energy bill. But here's the deal: effective as this may be in the short run, people know when they are being pressed, and they very often resent it. Operating this way can provoke the psychological phenomenon known as reactance. This is when people dig their heels in even further to resist the course of action you're pressuring them to take simply because they don't like to feel pushed.

Another form of pressure tactics is when you manipulate the flow of information to your target. This could take the form of deceptive advertising or presenting a carefully curated set of information that is designed to prompt someone to take action they otherwise wouldn't. This can certainly work to alter people's behavior, as chronicled extensively in books like Robert Cialdini's classic *Influence*, published in 1984. But beware. A good rule of thumb is to ask yourself, "Would I feel okay if someone used this pressure tactic on me?" If the answer is no, then you should remember you are operating outside the "green zone" shown in the Spectrum of Interpersonal Dynamics chart earlier in the chapter. You might feel justified in playing hardball for the sake of the greater good, but don't kid yourself into believing what you are doing is truly changing hearts and minds. Chances are, when you apply a pressure tactic, the best you'll get is compliance. This means you'll never be able to let up the pressure, so you haven't really found a stable solution. For a philanthropist, this likely means you are going to have to keep spending money continuously to keep the pressure on.

6. Never Initiate Violence—
Use it Only to Defend against Violent Aggression
and Abuse When Nothing Else Will Work

Unfortunate as it may be, when it comes to relationships between people, violence is a reality in our world. Even though this may be the last thing on your mind when it comes to gearing up your giving, the arena of philanthropy and social change is not magically exempt from this most extreme form of interpersonal dynamics.

Defining terms is important here. *Violence is not just physical.* There are instances of "callout" culture in the field of philanthropy and social change involving public attacks on someone's reputation that are experienced as a form of violence by those on the receiving end. Perhaps such violence may be justified when it is the only way to stop abuse that is persisting outside the reach of the conventional justice system, but this is tricky, subjective territory.

You probably have your own philosophy about when, if ever, it's acceptable to engage in violence. Guided by the insights of activist and author adrienne maree brown, my own belief is that violence is something we should never initiate against another person. At the same time, we are not obliged to suffer violence and abuse against ourselves or others without defending ourselves forcibly, particularly when there is no other way of avoiding immediate harm.

The key takeaway is to check yourself. Hard-edged, coercive tactics may verge into violence in the experience of those on the receiving end. Don't initiate violence unless you truly have no other choice to protect yourself and others from immediate, overwhelming harm.

FIVE SKILL-BUILDING TOOLS FOR STEPPING UP YOUR POSITIVE PRESENCE IN DIFFICULT CONVERSATIONS

If you want to engage effectively with others as you gear up your giving, it's important to understand why collaboration and co-creation are so valuable, particularly when it comes to lasting systems change. We've just gone over a conceptual framework that makes this point. But understanding these concepts is not the same as having the skills to implement them in your interactions with others, especially when the stakes are high.

Fortunately, we can draw on over fifty years of research and practice to upgrade our interpersonal communication skills. Much of this work centers on the foundational contributions of Harvard professor Chris Argyris, who developed the field of "action science" in the 1970s. His ongoing research over the next forty years deeply influenced a wide array of other theorists and practitioners, including pioneers in systems thinking like Peter Senge and the founding faculty of the Harvard Negotiation Program as well as Diana McLain Smith, Robert Putnam, and Philip McArthur of Action Design LLC. Another notable contributor is psychologist Marshall Rosenberg, author of *Nonviolent Communication*.

The payoff from all of this field-building work over the past fifty years is a set of practical skills for communicating more effectively in high-stakes situations. It's not an exaggeration to say these skills are truly a breakthrough with profound potential significance for all of us. Over the decades, many thousands of people have been trained in these techniques, yet they still remain largely outside mainstream use. Why? Because we are going up against millions of years of evolutionary psychology here. We are hardwired to be emotionally reactive and zero-sum in our interactions with others.

The good news is that with practice and commitment, you can rewire yourself. I encourage you to seek out the many resources, materials, and training opportunities available through institutions like the Harvard Negotiation Program, Action Design, and the Center for Nonviolent Communication. For now, I'll share an overview of five key tools that are a powerful foundation for building your skills as an empathetic and collaborative problem-solver.

Tool 1: Fight-or-Flight Systems Check

This is about taking stock of the emotional intensity of the issues you are dealing with in any given interaction. How ready are you and the other person to engage resourcefully and respectfully? How likely is either one of you to get triggered into an emotionally intense "fight or flight" reaction? This is where it can be helpful to remember the seven universal human needs we discussed in Chapter 2: security, novelty, social status, social connection, social contribution, self-evolution, and self-transcendence. Is either one of you struggling to meet any of these core psychological needs in this interaction? If so, these are the parts of the conversation in which that fight-or-flight brain is most likely to take over the controls and send you or the other person into an emotional overdrive.

The techniques that follow will help you identify when your defensive instincts are getting activated and help you reset yourself to a more resourceful stance.

- **Take a pulse check. Literally.** Practice getting in touch with the signals your body is sending you during challenging conversations. Learn to spot when you are going into fight-or-flight mode based on your own biofeedback, whether it's a racing pulse, a flushed face, or that tense feeling in the pit of your stomach.
- **Play for time.** When you feel your body going into fight-or-flight mode, take this as a cue to slow down the interaction. If at all possible, ask for time to process and take a break. If you can't pause the interaction, give your critical-thinking faculties some time to reemerge by asking questions rather than speaking. Do whatever you can to delay your response until the neurochemical flood of your fight-or-flight response has had time to ebb. Your defensive activation is temporary. You can let those powerful signals flow through your nervous system and get to a more resourceful, calm, and connected place on the other side. You can also practice in advance by rehearsing a difficult conversation ahead of time. This can help take the edge off your defensive response in the moment.
- **Name it to tame it.** Simply identifying the emotions you are experiencing can be a powerful way to begin shifting gears from your primitive, reactive brain to your higher-level faculties. The more you acknowledge what you are feeling, the more quickly you can let these emotions pass through and get to a more resourceful place from which to engage in collaborative problem-solving. This

is why the technique of asking the other party to name their concerns is so powerful—by acknowledging what we are experiencing, we can calm ourselves down much more quickly. Try this with a four-year-old who is in full spate, and you'll see just how quickly the crying stops, the flushed face settles down, and the creative brain switches back on.

Tool 2: Left-Hand Column/Right-Hand Column

The idea with this tool is that we can learn a great deal by deconstructing problematic conversations after the fact, comparing what was actually said with our unspoken thoughts and feelings. This tool was originally developed by Chris Argyris and Donald Schon in their 1974 book *Theory in Practice* and popularized by Peter Senge of Harvard Business School in his 1990 bestseller *The Fifth Discipline* and Diana McLain Smith (a colleague of both Argyris and Senge).

The technique is simple. Divide a sheet of paper into two columns. In the right-hand column, do the best you can to reconstruct a transcript of a significant conversation that did not turn out the way you had hoped. Make it read like a screenplay, with dialogue alternating between the characters. Label this right-hand column "What was said."

Label the left-hand column "What I was thinking and feeling but not saying." Here, add in any unspoken thoughts and feelings across from the corresponding portion of the spoken conversation in the right-hand column.

Here's a quick sample of what this looks like:

What I Was Thinking and Feeling But Not Saying	What Was Actually Said
	Me: Thanks for agreeing to sit down and talk about the path forward on this project.
Ouch, here we go again with her objections. She's clearly got a hidden agenda.	Joan: I'm always happy to learn more, though based on what you shared before, I'm not sure I can agree to what you're proposing.
What do I have to do to get through to her? I can't believe I have to go through this whole thing all over again.	Me: I understand you have reservations, and I'm hoping we can address those concerns because everybody else is ready to go, and there's a big chance we'll lose months of work if we don't move forward.

The key point of this tool is to give yourself the opportunity to reflect on your own unspoken thoughts and feelings. You don't want to accept these thoughts and feelings as the "truth"—you want to critically evaluate them instead. Ask yourself for evidence: how do you know that thought is true—can you really be sure? What possibilities would open up if you didn't believe that thought or if you chose a different interpretation of the situation? If that were the case, what feelings might you experience instead?

With practice, as you develop greater facility for understanding and interpreting your thoughts and feelings, you can develop a greater ability to productively communicate the key aspects of this inner experience and say them out loud. The idea is not to blurt out everything that's going on in your left-hand column. It could well be that there are ego-driven, ill-considered thoughts and highly reactive, momentary emotions going on inside you. Communicating your entire stream of consciousness to the other person usually doesn't advance the interaction toward productive collaboration. After all, *you* don't have to believe every thought that passes through your own mind or amplify every passing emotion you experience, so you certainly don't need to ask others to tune into your unexamined inner stream in its entirety.

Instead, sift through that inner stream, and identify the helpful thoughts and the processed feelings that can advance mutual understanding with the other person. As you get more practiced with this tool, you may find you are able to sort through your left-hand column during the conversation and communicate your "essential unsaids" to the other person in the moment. When you are starting out building this skill, you may find that you need to revisit the conversation at a later time. Either way, when you begin to share your key thoughts and feelings more fully and constructively, you've taken a major step forward in effective communication.

Tool 3: I-Messages

This is a specific way to communicate what might otherwise be left unsaid. Originally developed by the American psychologist

Thomas Gordon in the late 1950s, the purpose is to maximize the likelihood that you will get the other person to respond from a place of resourcefulness rather than defensiveness.

This tool can be particularly useful when you know in advance that you need to communicate something challenging to another person—something that could trigger one or both of you into a fight-or-flight emotional reaction. The idea is that you prepare your I-message in advance, before either of you gets into a heightened state. An I-message is a sentence that follows a specific, three-part formula. Here are the steps:

1. "When _____
   _____
   _____ happens
   (*describe only the factual circumstances at issue without judgment or editorializing*)

2. I feel _____
   _____
   _____
   (*describe your state of mind: what you are feeling inside yourself when this happens*)

3. because _____
   _____
   _____."
   (*describe which of your needs are at stake in this situation and how the circumstances in question are impacting your ability to meet these needs*)

4. Stop. Don't say anything else. Wait as long as it takes for the other person to respond. Listen deeply for the other person's feelings and needs as well as any requests they are making of you to help them meet their needs.

   After the other person has responded, you can take an optional bonus step, doing your best to make a collaborative proposal that meets both of your needs.

5. "Could it work for both of us if _____

   _____

   _____?"

   (do your best to make a collaborative proposal that meets both of your needs)

As you try this out, bear in mind that when you mention someone else directly, assuming the best of their motives helps avoid triggering defensiveness. Here's an example of what this might look like for a grantee communicating with a donor:

> *When your foundation asks my organization to report on a whole new set of metrics, I feel frustrated and overwhelmed because we already have three separate reporting requirements from the other three funders of this same project, and each time we have to produce a new set of reports, it takes staff time away from actually carrying out the project and producing the results we all care about in the field.*

Tool 4: Ladder of Understanding

This is a tool to use when you can't understand how someone else could see something so differently. What could they possibly be thinking? Perhaps not surprisingly, a great way to get insight about someone else's conclusions is to start by more closely examining your own!

Originally developed as the "Ladder of Inference" by Chris Argyris and also labeled the "Ladder of Reflection" by Diana McLain Smith in her book *Elephant in the Room*, I prefer to call this tool the "Ladder of Understanding." Whatever name you choose, it provides a framework for making clear the chain of reasoning that leads us from objective, observable facts all the way to value judgments about what is good and bad, right and wrong. The key insight here is that our brains work very quickly, and it's common to jump immediately from our observation of a situation all the way to a value judgment without even being conscious of our thought process in between.

It can be helpful here to remember Chapter 7's discussion of critical thinking—as human beings, we are prone to all kinds of cognitive biases. The kicker is that we can't see these blind spots, so we trust our own thought process more than we should. This tendency can add fuel to the fire in our highest-stakes interactions. We often have a high degree of confidence that our understanding of the situation is spot on, so we also believe that any right-thinking person would understand things the same way. This means we are quick to attribute bad motives if someone claims to see things differently.

What's the antidote? Slow down enough to walk yourself backward through all the steps (and assumptions) you took to reach your final conclusion, starting from your initial observations. Then co-create a new ladder of understanding with the other person, one step at a time.

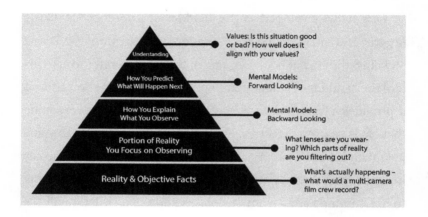

Let's dig a bit deeper to see how this works. The ground the ladder is resting on is reality and objective facts. The first step up the ladder is the portion of reality you actually observe. A lot of times we don't record reality objectively; we focus on only a portion of what actually happened, so our understanding of objective reality is already narrowed.

The next step up the ladder is how you explain what you observed to yourself. We all rely on mental models to explain why things happened in the way we observed. The step beyond that is that we very often want to predict what will happen next. Here, again, we draw on preexisting mental models. We are

MONEY WITH MEANING

typically deeply attached to our mental models and often not even aware we are using them. For example, many of us have a deeply entrenched mental model that we can predict the behavior of our whole economy based on the idea that individual people reliably act to advance their own self interests regardless of what is best for others. This is the fundamental model for classic economics and Adam Smith's "invisible hand." Often, we carry around these mental constructs unconsciously, and we cling to them even when contrary evidence emerges, such as survey research suggesting 50 percent or more of the population have a "pro-social" orientation and are willing to sacrifice gains for themselves for the sake of others getting what they need.[23]

The final rung of the ladder is our conclusion, where we form an overall understanding of the situation and make a judgment about whether it is aligned with our values. Is it good, bad, or indifferent?

Here's how to put this tool to use in practical terms when you reach a sticking point in a high-stakes conversation:

Step 1: Figure out which rung you are on. Are you still fairly low down on the ladder, say at the stage of observing what's going on around you? Or are you at the top of your ladder? Have you already formed a harsh judgment of someone else because you think you fully understand the situation and you believe their actions are not in accord with your values?

Step 2: Evaluate your reasoning by walking back down the ladder, step by step, until you get all the way back to objective reality. Look for any unwarranted or inaccurate assumptions you might have made in your original reasoning process.

Step 3: Rebuild the ladder in a conversation with your counterparty, explicitly communicating about each step as you go. Narrate your assumptions as you move up the ladder, all the way to a shared understanding that is consistent with values that you both share.

It might seem hard to imagine using this tool in practice, especially if you are really at odds with someone else and the conversation has gotten heated. As you develop greater facility with these tools, you may find that combining them is really effective. For example, you can use Step 5 of an I-message to suggest using the Ladder of Understanding as a mutually beneficial step forward: "Could it work for both of us if we took a pause and shared our thinking about how we each reached our point of view? Maybe we can peel the onion here and see if we might each have missed something along the way."

Tool 5: Advocacy and Inquiry: Balancing Energy and Empathy

How well are you balancing advocacy and inquiry in your high-stakes conversations? This is the question behind another key tool pioneered by Chris Argyris. Effective interactions require a balance between sharing your views clearly and listening empathetically to others. If this balance gets skewed one way or the other, it's that much harder to land in the green zone for collaborative problem-solving.

Becoming familiar with this tool and practicing it is important because in a real high-stakes conversation, we often find it very hard to achieve this balance between inquiry and advocacy. A great way to build your skills here is to reconstruct conversations that went awry using the Left-Hand Column/Right-Hand Column tool. Not only can you use that tool to surface your unspoken thoughts and feelings, but you can also use it to check for the balance of advocacy and inquiry in the conversation.

Start by looking at the level of energy you are bringing to the conversation. How actively are you advocating for your own views, and how actively are you inquiring about the other person's views?

	Low-Energy Inquiry	High-Energy Inquiry
High-Energy Advocacy	**Educating** at best vs. **Insisting** at worst	**Co-Creation** at best vs. **Endless Deliberation** at worst
Low-Energy Advocacy	**Watching** at best vs. **Withdrawing** at worst	**Asking** at best vs. **Auditing** at worst

As this chart illustrates, there's an opportunity for at least some form of positive interaction in each of these four quadrants, even though high-energy inquiry combined with high-energy advocacy yields the greatest benefits. For example, when you are mediating between colleagues, it may be appropriate for you to dial down both your advocacy and your inquiry and simply play the role of watching their interaction. Similarly, when you are tasked with interviewing an expert as part of a research project, it makes sense for you to focus your energy on inquiry and not on sharing your own views. But if you are seeking a lasting, co-created solution, you'll need to bring a balance of energized advocacy and inquiry to the interaction.

You can also see that in each quadrant, there is a less-functional possibility. For example, if you show up in a high-stakes conversation by strongly articulating your own views without doing much inquiry about the other person's views, you might end up not getting through at all and be stuck fruitlessly insisting on your views. So, how do you avoid the worst-case ends of the spectrum? By ensuring that you are bringing empathy for the other person into the interaction.

Bringing empathy to your advocacy means you state your views in a way the other person can really understand—you are empathizing with their experience as a listener and fully narrating your own reasoning process so they don't have to struggle to fill in the blanks. Bringing empathy to your inquiry means you start out by asking for the other person's views with genuine curiosity, actively seeking insights around what you might not see yourself. As the chart below illustrates, engaging in empathetic advocacy and inquiry is the way you can co-create solutions that have the greatest likelihood of lasting.

	Self-Centered Inquiry	Empathetic Inquiry
Self-Centered Advocacy	**Get on Board or Else** Trust me, this is exactly what we should do. You agree, right?	**Mixed Messages** Trust me—this is exactly what we should do. What do you think? Am I missing anything important?
Empathetic Advocacy	**Hard Sell** Here's what I'm thinking makes the most sense for the following reasons. And here's why I believe all other options come up short. Don't you see how nothing else is going to work?	**Co-created Solutions** What do you see as the best path forward—and why does that approach make the most sense to you? With your ideas in mind, I'd like to share what I'm thinking makes the most sense for the following reasons—please tell what I might be missing from your perspective.

It takes time to incorporate these five tools into your repertoire because these skills go against our most primitive fight-or-flight wiring. This means they don't come naturally; they have to be learned and practiced. But the reward is worth it: the opportunity to innovate and collaborate precisely when we are otherwise most likely to get hijacked by our own fight-or-flight response. This is how you truly live up to the commitment of treating others with consideration not contempt, and in turn bring both greater joy and impact to your giving.

GETTING BETTER

Pushing Past Your Comfort Zone

"What got you here, won't get you there."

—MARSHALL GOLDSMITH

Maybe you've got your personal growth and self-care routine dialed in just the way you like it. Maybe you think that gearing up your giving should be about focusing on others, not yourself.

But let me ask you something. Remember that rating you gave yourself way back in Chapter 1? How are you feeling about the impact of your giving so far on a scale of one to ten? And what about your sense of personal fulfillment and joy in your giving on that same one-to-ten scale? If you're already a ten and a ten, that's great! But chances are, there's room for improvement in either the impact of your giving or your own sense of fulfillment as you do it.

Why? Because your fullest potential as a human being and a change agent is almost always outside your current comfort zone.

What's more, the vast majority of us are still functioning on a kludged-together version of humanity's original mental operating system, something that is optimized for a simpler, bygone world of prehistoric fight-or-flight survival by individuals and small groups.

How do we meet the challenge of finding both joy and impact in the time and place we actually live in? This is an increasingly interconnected world full of wickedly complex problems that we can neither fight our way out of nor run away from. We are called to evolve ourselves and our own level of consciousness—our own way of being—in order to give joyfully and impactfully. We are called to change the world for real, and that process begins with ourselves.

ARE YOU READY TO EXPAND YOUR CURRENT PSYCHOLOGICAL RANGE?

Let's begin by exploring your baseline comfort zone and then consider what the next level in your growth might be. A great place to start is with a framework from cognitive behavioral psychology. This tells us that your *state of mind* in any given moment is determined by the intersection of three factors: your thoughts, your feelings, and your actions.

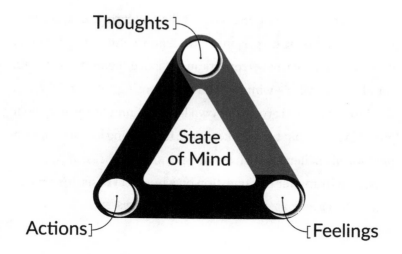

You can think of your "psychological range" as being made up of all the various states of mind that you experience over time. Within your personal psychological range, chances are you have some home turf, or a comfort zone made up of one or more states of mind that you tend to experience more often than others. There's a good reason for this tendency toward following routine mental patterns. Without some default mental patterns, navigating a world crammed with choices from one moment to the next would be overwhelming.

It's possible you even have one or more go-to mindsets. Let's define a mindset as a state of mind that you gravitate to so repeatedly that it becomes a habitual frame of reference—an orientation from which you approach much of your life.

As you gear up your giving, there's a good chance the mindsets that have served you well in your life to date may not get you where you want to go in this arena. What if the secret to your success so far has been taking no prisoners in a highly competitive industry where quarterly earnings reports and balance sheets make it plain for all to see who's winning and who's losing? How might you need to stretch and grow your own habits of mind to gear up your giving in a way that truly makes sense for tackling long-term, complex social challenges such as chronic homelessness? If you want to be able to answer this question on a practical basis, it's time to take a closer look at your mental operating system.

FIVE FUNDAMENTAL STATES OF MIND

Let's dig a little deeper to explore five states of mind that almost all of us experience at one time or another in our lives:

- **Scarcity**: When you are in this state of mind, your overwhelming concern is that you won't be able to get what you need. Your focus is on doing whatever it takes to get your needs fulfilled. There are certainly times in life when you need to operate from this survival-focused frame, such as when you are caught in the immediate crisis of a natural disaster. But when your survival instincts kick in, they typically narrow your field of vision. When you are in this mental mode, your choices often appear binary. *Either I do what it takes to meet my needs, or I lose out.* It's costly to let a scarcity state of mind creep in when it's not truly necessary. When you are caught up in this mental mode, you may act in ways that violate your own values to get what you need. This mindset comes in at least two forms:

- **Individualist mode**, in which your focus is solely on your individual needs.
- **Loyalty mode**, in which your focus is on meeting the needs of your group, family, organization, or whatever unit of people you define as "yours."

• **Externally directed:** When you are in this state of mind, you are focused on figuring out the "rules of the game." What do others expect and value in you and your behavior? You are looking to others for clues and cues about how best to shape your thoughts, feelings, and actions in order to fit in and find success within a given social order. This state of mind is an essential part of our socialization as a species. We would never be able to live together in groups and cooperate if we didn't have a large part of our mental wiring available to process all the signals we get from those around us and shape our behavior accordingly. There are several different forms of this mode:

- **Fitting in:** You are focused on figuring out what is socially acceptable and meeting that norm. You want to be just like everyone else, to "go with the flow" and "run with the pack."
- **Getting by:** You don't necessarily embrace a given social norm, nor do you want to deal with the consequences of openly going your own way. You focus on performing at the

absolute minimum threshold of acceptability. Ever worked somewhere with a dress code you chafed against?

- ○ **Standing out**: You want to win the approval of others by performing over and above the norm. You want to distinguish yourself in the eyes of those whose judgment you respect. Phi Beta Kappa, anyone?

- **Executive**: When you are in this state of mind, you are focused on formulating plans, identifying and acquiring key resources, and enlisting others to help you accomplish your goals. This is the state of mind that many of us rely on to exercise "leadership" in the conventional sense. There are a few versions of the executive mode as well.

  - ○ **Manager**: This is about telling others what to do and having them execute exactly to your directions. Remember the distinction between simple, complicated, and complex challenges we talked about in Chapter 8? Manager mode is great when the task at hand is relatively simple and the causal chain is clear. Your job is to make sure that people have clear directions and perform their assigned duties reliably.

  - ○ **Engineer**: This is a matter of putting together a complicated, step-by-step process where failure at any point leads to failure overall. Tight control is key to make sure everyone does their part and the process functions as specified. Bursts of creativity under pressure are also key when something does go wrong— think Apollo 13. This is often a highly functional leadership mode when the task at hand is complicated. It involves many precise, sequential steps in a causal chain from A to Z.

- **Conductor:** In this mode, you are attuned to the individual voices, qualities, and attributes of others, and you seek to get things done by bringing a team together in the most harmonious possible way. The sum is greater than the parts, and you appreciate possibilities for collaboration with an artist's sensibility. Notwithstanding the artistry of this mode, at the end of the day, like an orchestra conductor, you are still clearly in charge. Your responsibility is to deliver a result for a simple or complicated challenge drawing on a bounded ecosystem of actors over whom you have at least formal authority. Think of university presidents or legislative leaders at the top of their game.

- **Evolutionary:** When you are in this state of mind, you see your own growth and adaptation as a key way to address challenges and find fulfillment. You operate on the premise that the best way to meet your own needs and serve others is by shifting your own approach to be more flexible and creative in how you pursue your aims. You are even willing to reconsider which aims you find most valuable. You tend to focus most on exercising positive influence rather than formal authority. The nature of the challenges you tackle is often complex, where there is no reliable formula for achieving a solution in advance. Think about Nelson Mandela and the evolution in personal outlook during his twenty-five years in prison that lay behind his success establishing South Africa's first National Unity government.

- **Self-Transcending**: When you are in this state of mind, you are focused on looking beyond the limits of yourself as the key actor. Some of the questions you ask yourself seem almost metaphysical: *What larger truth or whole is seeking expression through me? What larger systems am I a part of, and what leverage do I have to transform these systems through my own actions and by coming together with others? What ripples can I help set in motion whose ultimate impact I can't even predict or perceive?* Your problem-solving and leadership in this mode are focused on taking yourself out of the equation. *How can I develop others? How can I best position others to address this challenge above and beyond anything I do myself?* Think of spiritual leaders such as the Dalai Lama when looking for inspiration or examples of this.

TAKING STOCK: WHICH STATES OF MIND HAVE SERVED YOU BEST SO FAR?

Which of these states of mind do you tend to experience the most? We experience all these states of mind, sometimes dramatically so, from one moment to the next. What's the secret of your success so far? Have any states of mind become so well patterned for you that they have crossed over to become mindsets, or comfortable lenses through which you tend to view the world?

Assessing your own state of mind can be difficult. If you are in the grips of a scarcity or externally directed state of mind, you may not have the mental space to notice your own thoughts and feelings in the moment. Likewise, if your go-to mode is an executive mindset, you may move through life so focused on getting things done that you haven't taken much time to build up your skills for "getting up on the balcony" and critically examining yourself. If you want some help assessing your mental modes, there are a number of options, from tracking down an interviewer trained in Kegan and Lahey's "Scale of Mental Complexity" to the STAGES Matrix and its online assessment.

But without getting hung up about where you are starting from, the most important question is *where do you want to go from here?*

WHICH STATES OF MIND WILL SERVE YOU BEST AS YOU GEAR UP YOUR GIVING?

As you gear up your giving, it's perfectly natural for you to draw on the mental modes that have served you well in your life to date. For example, donors who are starting out sometimes adopt an externally directed mindset precisely because philanthropy is a relatively new field to them; they're looking to others to learn the ropes. It's understandable that you would initially look to others for cues and clues about how to think, feel, and act when it comes to your philanthropy, maybe at first by fitting in and over time by setting your sights on standing out in the eyes of others.

It's also natural for those looking to gear up their giving to draw significantly on their executive mindset. It's no surprise if a key reason you're in a position to be philanthropic in the first place is that you are good at analyzing challenges, making plans, and getting things done, whether in manager mode, conductor mode, or engineer mode. So, you may be naturally excited to bring your leadership experience and talent to bear on social challenges of your choosing. Let's get going on making the world a better place!

But if you want your giving to contribute to *lasting change* on the most-entrenched problems that most impact our shared future, you're going to need to cultivate at least one additional mindset, maybe two. For complex challenges in which solutions cannot be engineered in advance, you'll need to invest in your own growth and evolution to give in a way that truly makes sense for you and the larger world. This comes back to the distinction we made earlier between simple, complicated, and complex problems.

Complex problems are characterized by emergent, systemic dynamics. You can't achieve success by charting out a linear cause-and-effect solution in advance. One of the most critical misfires in philanthropy is a faulty diagnosis of the nature of the problem the philanthropist is working on. Too many philanthropists proceed as if the problem they are committed to addressing is simple or complicated at best. These are the types of problems for which an executive mindset is well suited. But what if the issue you want to address is actually a complex, emergent challenge? For example, if you are committed to addressing chronic homelessness in your home city, a significant part of your giving is going to involve backing folks on the front lines to identify promising pathways for emergent solutions. As you address one aspect of the challenge, such as mental health issues and substance dependency, you may find that new challenges arise. This can come in the form of opposition from residents in some neighborhoods who do not want homeless people relocated to their area. Rather than trying to specify every single step of the strategy in advance, you're going to have to be willing to adapt and evolve your approach over time. When you take on complexity, you have to be willing to embrace its messy, nonlinear nature. You have to be willing to adapt and evolve your own patterns of thoughts, feelings, and action in response to the system's emergent properties and convolutions. You will find yourself needing to call on not just your executive mindset modes but also an evolutionary state of mind.

This is why it's worth trying on an evolutionary state of mind and even a self-transcending state of mind when possible. These states of mind ultimately stem from an ability to trust that you can be flexible and adaptive enough to overcome any obstacles to meeting your own ego-driven needs as you carry out your giving. This frees you up to focus your highest and best self on maximizing your service to something larger than yourself.

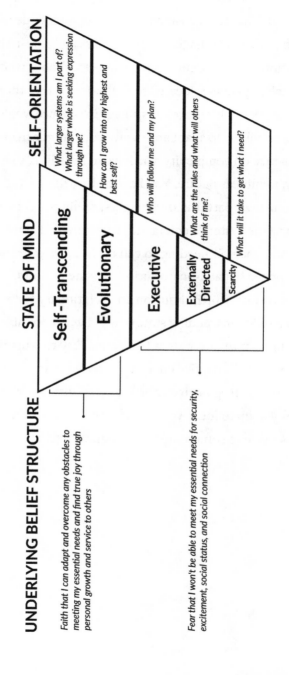

LOOKING AHEAD

What does it actually look like to lean into your own evolution and self-transcendence with giving back better in mind? The next chapter introduces a framework for personal growth that I've used extensively in my coaching practice with philanthropists, philanthropy advisors, and social entrepreneurs. These Seven Pillars of Personal Development for Change Agents are about building up the knowledge, skills, and mindset to show up as the most philanthropic, best version of yourself.

THE SEVEN PILLARS
OF PERSONAL
DEVELOPMENT

Stepping into Your
Full Potential as a Change Agent

"What you can be, you must be."

—ABRAHAM MASLOW

As we've just explored, translating money into meaning through your giving sometimes requires you to operate outside your comfort zone. This begins by acknowledging the role that fear can play as a powerful undercurrent in our giving. We fear we will feel guilty if we don't give back more and better. We fear that no matter how much we give, it won't be enough to make a real difference. We fear that we'll end up looking foolish and others won't appreciate or align themselves with our efforts. We may fear that grantees will waste our money and abuse our trust, or we may be afraid that what really matters to the world is our money, not our ideas and our full selves. We fear that we will be misunderstood and judged harshly, that we will fail, and that whatever we are trying to build will fall flat.

What will it take for you to set aside these fears in order to evolve and level up your giving? This chapter is here to help you answer that question by exploring seven key arenas for personal growth and learning. This is about switching the power source for your giving from fear to joy. As we walk through the Seven Pillars of Personal Development, I'll highlight one or two key practices for each pillar. If you want to dig into this more deeply, worksheets for each of these seven pillars are available at the book's website.

THE SEVEN PILLARS
OF PERSONAL DEVELOPMENT

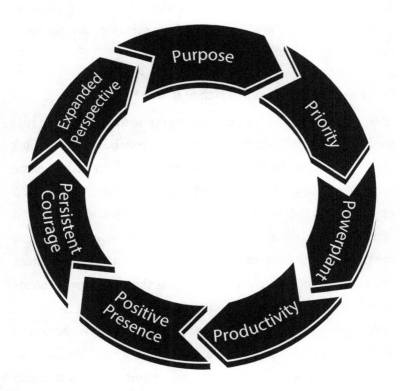

Pillar 1: Purpose

If you want to set yourself up for maximum fulfillment and impact, you need to start with clarity about your purpose in life. Here's why: we achieve fulfillment and impact in life by consistently acting in alignment with our highest selves. Without having clarity about who we aspire to be and the positive impact we are called to bring to the world, we can't be fully conscious of what it takes to act in alignment with that highest and best version of ourselves. Similarly, without knowing our purpose, we lose our sense of progress. That feeling of forward movement is vital for our sense of well-being in life!

Three Key Life Domains in which to Define Your Purpose

Clarity about your life's purpose begins with recognizing that we all have several distinct life domains. It may be helpful to think about yourself as having a distinct purpose within each of these areas. What do you call these different life areas? One common approach is to think in terms of work, family, and personal. A variant of this is to think in terms of energy, work, and love. These are the categories that Brian Johnson uses with all his resources at Optimize.me. I prefer to think of these three life areas in terms of impact, joy, and personal power plant.

Whatever terms you use, these three areas are interconnected. A life of extraordinary impact and joy rests on making purposeful investments in your personal power plant. That's what these Seven Pillars of Personal Development are all about.

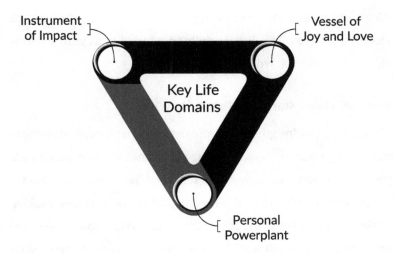

Instrument of Impact

Vessel of Joy and Love

Key Life Domains

Personal Powerplant

Essentially, getting clarity on your purpose in life is about discerning your highest calling in each of these three areas.

- What contribution are you called to make as an instrument of impact out in the world?
- What gifts of love, caring, and presence are you called to share with your family, friends, and broader community as a vessel of joy?
- In what ways are you called to grow and learn in order to show up more consistently as your best, most energized self?

Let's guide you through the process of producing a personal vision statement. This is an expression of your purpose that can serve as your North Star. Even if you've done something like this in the past, it's worth doing fresh right now. Just as our life circumstances change and evolve over time, so does the best version of ourselves. This is especially true for all of us with a strong calling to make the world a better place.

Personal Vision Statement Part 1: My What

Here's what we're going for: a short, one-paragraph statement describing your highest and best self. What kind of person are you at your best, and how is this reflected in the way you care for others and for yourself? What contribution do you love making in the world? What is the transformative change you are seeking to bring about? What standards do you hold yourself to in your care for others? What energy do you bring with you into the room? What are the roles and regular activities you own as a core part of your identity (e.g., I am a sister, a father, a thought leader, etc.)?

If you had to complete these sentences, what would you say?

My mission in life is _____

_____?

My whole life is about _____

_____?

Personal Vision Statement Part 2: My Why

Now, it's time to reflect on your personal *why*. Why are you moved to live your life in accordance with the vision you just laid out? What key experiences and feelings have influenced and shaped you to go after this vision with such passion and dedication? Acquiring clarity about the most powerful feelings, beliefs, and values that energize you is a gift worth giving yourself.

The Final Step

It's simple—print out your *what* and *why* vision statements, and put them someplace where you'll see them every day. Even better, read them out loud to yourself at least once a week. Before you plan your next week is a great time to reground yourself in the power of your personal vision.

Additional Resources

Creating a personal vision statement for yourself is a great foundational exercise for clarifying your purpose, and there are lots more resources to draw on at this book's website, including journaling prompts as well as the "Magic Genie" exercise.

Pillar 2: Priority

Having clear priorities about the actions you take is how you translate your purpose into progress each day. That feeling of tangible progress is absolutely vital to your sense of well-being as a change agent. The deeper your sense of purpose about making the world a better place, the more keenly you will feel out of alignment if you're not making progress toward this vision. This section will guide you through the process of dialing in your priorities, both as an instrument of impact for your mission in the world and as a vessel of joy for all those whose lives you touch.

What's Getting in the Way of Dialing In on Your Priorities?

Sometimes, a helpful starting point for setting your priorities can come from where you feel most stuck in your life. When we get stuck, we tend to get caught up in a negative mental loop. Often, when you are struggling to establish and act on your priorities, you'll find yourself getting bogged down in procrastination and busywork, suffering from a sense of exhaustion and overwhelm. I have found there are six patterns of thinking and feeling that often get in our way as change agents. In my coaching practice, we call these "obstructing angels" because these behaviors are *trying* to keep us safe, but they get in our way nonetheless.

The Six Obstructing Angels of Joy and Impact

When you lack clarity about your priorities, which of these barriers to impact and joy come into play in your life? What does focusing your time and energy on the wrong things cost you?

Three Key Life Domains in which to Set Your Priorities

It's important to define and communicate your purpose and priorities in all three major life domains (impact, joy, and your power plant). At this book's website, you can find three worksheets, one for each of these areas. Below, we'll walk through the questions that go along with setting your priorities for the impact domain of your life—you could call this your "mission" or "work" as well.

Identifying and Prioritizing Your Mission-Maximizing Output

1. What is your **ultimate vision for a better world**? What is true and flourishing in that world you dream to see, whether in your own lifetime or for children in coming generations?

2. Many factors will likely have to come together to bring this ultimate vision for the world into reality. What particular element of this change story is calling most for *your* service? What is your **arena of engagement** in pursuit of this ultimate vision, whether for now or for life? Is there a personal story or experience that leads you to focus on this arena of engagement?

3. What's the most **audacious measure of impact** in your chosen arena of engagement? What will be different when you and others have succeeded beyond your dreams within this arena and made the greatest possible contribution toward the ultimate vision for a better world you named in Question 1?

4. Within your chosen arena of engagement, what is the most important contribution for you to make toward the audacious measure of impact you named in Question 3? What is the *one* thing you can do such that by doing it, everything else on the path to achieving audacious impact becomes easier or even unnecessary? (Read Gary Keller's *The ONE Thing* for more on this.) Jim Collins introduced the idea of the "hedgehog concept" in his book *Good to Great* as a way to figure out exactly how to focus a business for unique success in a competitive market. Recall the "What" section from Chapter 3. Again, here is an adaptation of this idea for change agents. **Your *one* thing** is located at the intersection of the following four spheres: the root cause of the problem, the resource engine that can reliably bring money and other assets in to solve the problem, your passion, and your talent.

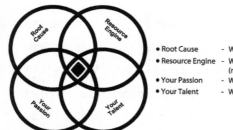

- Root Cause — What's causing the problem in your Arena of Engagement?
- Resource Engine — What can reliably provide money and other assets (not just your own!) to solve the problem?
- Your Passion — What do you love doing?
- Your Talent — What are you great at doing?

5. When you achieve success pursuing your one thing, how will you know? Brainstorm a list of the **lagging indicators** of your successful impact. These are the measures of success once you have achieved it.

6. How will you know you are on the right track? Brainstorm a list of the daily or weekly activities that constitute **leading indicators** of your successful impact.

7. From your list of leading indicators, which stand out as the most powerful contributors to your lagging indicators? This is your **mission-maximizing output** (**MMO**), the activities that truly move the needle most on the outcomes you value.

8. What is the next best step for you to prioritize your MMO on a daily and weekly basis? What percentage of your work time are you spending on producing your MMO now? See if you can start tracking this and gradually increase your MMO percentage from month to month. Any sustained improvement, however small, is incredibly valuable. This is because prioritizing the most powerful contributors to your most valued outcomes pays compound interest over time!

You can condense your answers into a one-page primer (available on this book's website) and go through the same exercise for setting your priorities around joy and love as well as your personal power plant.

Pillar 3: Personal Power Plant

When it comes to your personal energy, metaphors matter! Do you treat yourself like a battery or a power plant? When you think of yourself like a battery, chances are you're just trying to make it through the day before you run your charge down to zero. But as Brendon Burchard points out in *High Performance Habits*, when you think about yourself like a power plant, you have a lot more options for engineering your energy output. This helps you sustain your joy and your impact throughout the day. This is a fundamental shift in thinking that has dramatic implications for how you approach this vital arena of your life: your personal energy level.

Engineering Your Personal Power Plant: Sleep, Nutrition, Movement, and Mindfulness

1. Sleep: This is a big one. So many of us with a vision to change the world are literally falling asleep on the job. There is a lot of compelling and clear research showing that to be on your A game consistently, day in and day out, you need seven to eight hours of sleep on average. With the exception of a rare few, there's pretty much no way around this biological imperative.

Unfortunately, it's a lot harder to get this kind of restorative sleep than it was a generation or two ago. Our bodies just didn't evolve to live in an age of electric lighting, much less laptops, smartphones, and TV screens in our bedrooms. The result has been an outbreak of sleep-related health problems and productivity issues. The good news is that the world of sleep science has been making significant strides. Here are some of the best practices to follow (you can check out this book's website for a deeper dive):

- Pick a set wakeup time and stick with it as closely as you can for all seven days of the week. If something has to give, vary your bedtime.

- Use an Oura ring or other device that tracks your sleep quantity and quality. This kind of feedback can be invaluable in helping you dial in the practices that really lead to good sleep.
- Think about your sleep target in weekly terms of ninety-minute sleep cycles. Most people will find they achieve optimum performance at about thirty-five cycles, which is the equivalent of 7.5 hours per night. Don't try to get by on less than twenty-eight to thirty on a long-term basis.
- Food and drink sunset: Don't eat or drink anything within ninety minutes of your bedtime on a given night, and do what you can to progressively dim the light you are exposed to during this wind-down period.
- Digital sunset: Progressively step back from your smart-phone and other technology in the sixty to ninety minutes before bedtime. There are several reasons for this. First, you don't want to create stress you can't immediately resolve by checking emails and so on. Second, all that screen time is exposing you to light that tells your body not to slow down.
- Create a cool, dark, quiet place for sleep. Eliminate as much light, noise, clutter, and excessive heat from your sleeping environment as possible.
- Breathe right. This means breathing through your nose, not your mouth—yes, this means taping your mouth shut if that's what it takes!

- "Download your day" before you go to sleep. For me, this is about journaling for five minutes and taking another five to ten minutes to plan out my next day. I also close out the day by doing a simple meditation routine for ten minutes as the last thing I do before getting into bed. Half the time, I am already on the verge of sleep in the last few minutes of that meditation.

- Give yourself permission to take naps and meditation breaks. If you get less than the number of sleep cycles you want on a given night, you can make them up with naps and restful meditation on subsequent days. It's actually totally okay to sleep on the job intentionally! Don't be the one who's falling asleep in the afternoon meeting by accident.

2. Nutrition: How we feed and nourish our bodies has so much to do with the level of energy we bring to our mission and to our loved ones. Almost all of us are carrying some emotional baggage in our relationship with our bodies and in our relationship with food. Healing starts here. The ultimate value for taking your nutrition to the next level is to find more joy and more energy. You'll also enjoy a greater sense of alignment and integration with your own body and the world around you.

There are so many resources you can draw on here, so I won't attempt to provide a comprehensive set of recommendations. I will share the guiding principles that I've found most helpful as I've dialed in this part of my own power plant.

Foundational Ideas:

- A calorie is not a calorie. The basic math we've been taught about weight gain and weight loss doesn't actually add up.
- Food can be medicine for your metabolism.
- Your metabolism is an *amazing* biological machine, and it can evolve with you over time.
- Your microbiome matters hugely to your metabolic health—eating in tune with your body has a lot to do with farming your gastrointestinal flora.
- You are playing a long game, so remember that no one meal and no one day makes or breaks anything.
- Experiment, attune, and enjoy!

Some Specifics to Try:

- Bring mindfulness to what and how you eat. Pause while eating to attune to signals of hunger and fullness. What tastes and sensations are you really enjoying? What tastes and sensations are less appealing?
- Listen to your body and use data. Get bloodwork done, and figure out if you have any deficiencies or other medical conditions that food and supplements can address.
- If you really want to have "rules," try to keep them as simple and flexible as possible. For example:
  - Eat more real food and less processed food.
  - Drink more water and less sugar.

3. Movement: Notice that I'm not calling this "exercise." Exercise is key to engineering your power plant, but it's actually only one component of the broader category of physical movement. Human beings evolved to be on our feet; we evolved to be in motion throughout our waking day. When it comes to engineering your power plant and creating energy within yourself, one of the most important things is to put your body in motion throughout the day. Far too many of us deplete ourselves in the mistaken belief that buckling down to work in long marathons is the most efficient way to operate. In reality, to keep your power plant operating at a high, sustained energy output, you should get up and move for at least several minutes every hour. And yes, this does mean getting up and moving around in the middle of a multi-hour meeting! Yes, it does mean stretching and jumping up and down with your shoulders hanging loose and your eyes closed. There are lots of great micro-exercises you can engage in on brief breaks like this. Rather than reaching for another cup of coffee when you feel yourself flagging, get up and move!

Some general principles:

- Movement matters—it's not just exercise. Don't just work out once a day and sit around the rest of the time. Regular movement is key to generating energy and focus.
- This seems like common sense, but it's worth saying: movement and nutrition need to be in balance for you to maintain a stable weight and a stable level of energy.

That doesn't mean your cycles of nutrition and movement are on the same periodicity. With movement, you don't want to have one giant spike and flatline the rest of the day, even though that might work to help you maintain a stable weight. That's not the only thing to pay attention to. When it comes to nutrition, there can be value in creating longer spaces when you are not eating anything, especially in the evening and overnight. This gives your body a chance to process and balance body chemistry, and it's how our bodies were designed to work over thousands and thousands of years. As bestselling author Shawn Stevenson states in his 2020 book *Eat Smarter*, "The truth is, intermittent fasting isn't a new invention—breakfast is."

- In addition to regular movement, you also need genuine exercise, or movement that is more intense from a cardiovascular standpoint. There are so many options here, so why not find something that has mindfulness benefits too or that you find enjoyable in some other way?

- Make your movement doable. Use habit-formation science to help you out here. Set triggers, remove obstacles, and otherwise engineer your day both for exercise and regular movement. Look for opportunities to accomplish tasks in ways that involve moving your body for a few minutes.

- In your working day, look for calls you can take or receive while walking. The world won't come to an end if you get off video and just walk around while talking!

4. Mindfulness: Critical thinking and deep work is the most energy-intensive activity you engage in at any point in your day. You need to treat your mind like a muscle; it is something that you work out and that you rest. When it comes to mindfulness, there are four practices that I'd recommend in particular:

- **Morning priming**: What you do first thing in the morning really matters. You have the opportunity to set your energy positively for the rest of the day. This is a great place to invest in a regular practice that Tony Robbins has memorably called "morning priming." Ideally, you do this first thing in the morning, right after you get up and before you get deep into your day. There's still tremendous value to be had even if you can only fit this in a bit later in your morning. There's lots of room for experimentation and personal creativity with this. Here's the ten-minute routine I use. It combines Tony Robbins's framework with some elements of my own, as well as additions and adaptations from Brendon Burchard and Napoleon Hill.
  - First three minutes: I stand up and place both hands on my heart. I spend three minutes thinking of what I am grateful for as specifically and visually as possible, often by recalling visualizations of moments from the previous day.
  - Next three minutes: I stand with my palms face up and with my hands to either side. I envision and feel myself filling up with God's healing presence from the soles of my feet all the

way up to the crown of my head. Then, I begin to remember the needs of others and pray on their behalf. I hold my hands up on either side of the center of my chest and visualize all that positive energy is radiating outward from my chest, passing between my hands in a beam of light and reaching out to touch those for whom I am praying.

- Next ninety seconds: I do three sets of thirty reps, rapidly inhaling through my nose and exhaling through my mouth while raising and lowering my arms over my head in time with each breath. I take a deep diaphragmatic breath between each of the three sets.

- Next ninety seconds: I repeat my daily directive affirmation out loud to myself, speaking with emphasis and conviction and engaging my whole body, using gestures and physical movement. Don't worry if you think this makes you look like you're talking to yourself. This is you and your subconscious really getting deep into it!

- Final minute: I ask and answer a set of daily questions, such as, "Where can my full presence make the biggest difference in my personal life today?" and, "At the end of this day, what must be true for me to feel like I've lived in alignment with my best self and made the biggest contribution I could?"

- **Downloading your day through journaling**: Keeping a journal is a valuable daily practice with benefits that pay compound interest. If you want to go further and faster in your quest to change the world, taking a little time to reflect on your experience along the way is a powerful accelerant. As a daily practice, this doesn't need to take more than ten minutes. If you're just getting started and think you don't have the time, work your way up—start with just two to three minutes. The rule for this journal is that it is positively oriented. This is not the place to work out your inner demons. I love the advice about journaling that Warren Rustand shares in his 2020 book *The Leader Within Us*. He suggests you write as if some-day your grandkids could read it and get to know you after you're gone—even though you are actually writing it for yourself.

- **Evening meditation:** What you do right before bed really matters. You and your unconscious brain and body are going to spend the next seven to eight hours in an extended period of recovery, dialog, and problem-solving. Establishing a regular practice of evening meditation is a great way to set yourself up for a restful night. If you are new to meditation, not knowing where to start can seem daunting. Let's keep it simple. The main thing is just to get started. A number of people I know, myself included, found meditation to be particularly challenging at first. Trying to quiet your mind in a systematic, focused way for the first time can be a humbling experience. Your mind does not know how to shut up! This is because you haven't ever tried to train it to do this. Imagine if you let a little puppy grow into a big dog before you ever tried to teach it how to behave. The key is to be kind, forgiving, and patient with yourself while also maintaining the expectation that you will eventually gain more control over how you focus your mind. There are a host of great resources out there to help you with this, whether they are guided meditation apps like Headspace or the video course offered by the Hindu priest Dandapani (learn. dandapani.org). Brendon Burchard has a simple guided meditation that is easy to find with an internet search as well. If you find that you are really struggling to quiet your mind and release anxiety, I would recommend the progressive relaxation and stress-clearing procedure outlined in Chapter 3 of *Your Hands Can Heal You* by Steven Co.

- **Breathwork throughout the day:** This is about taking small pauses whenever you want to bring more presence and intentionality to yourself in the moment. You can do this simply by taking a few deep, diaphragmatic breaths. Breathe into your belly for a count of five. Hold for two, and exhale for eight. There's striking research about how daily breathwork like this can reduce the level of stress-response hormones such as cortisol in your blood. Two of these breaths take only thirty seconds, and nobody around you even has to know that you just reset yourself. If you want to go deeper here, James Nestor's book *Breath* is an outstanding guide to both the science and the practice of breathwork.

Pillar 4: Productivity

One of the most powerful boosts to productivity is to start your working day with deep focus on your highest priority. This is why productivity is the fourth pillar of personal development. It builds on having your first three pillars pretty well dialed in: knowing your purpose, knowing your priorities, and having an energized power plant. With this foundation in place, start your day with a block of deep work on the mission-maximizing output you identified as your top priority. Do this before you start consuming content—before you get into your email, before you get into social media, and before you read the news. Create your MMO first! Pomodoros work well as a unit of production. These are twenty-five-minute work sprints in which you commit to focus exclusively on banging out as much work as you can with no distractions. This is followed by a five-minute break when you can do whatever you want. If you are just starting out and don't feel like you can commit to starting every workday with a twenty-five-minute block of deep work, shorten the time to whatever length you know you can accomplish even on your worst day.

The science of habit formation shows us there are big benefits in making your routine as similar as possible from one day to the next. This means you don't have to make decisions each day about whether to do your deep work block. Likewise, tracking how many deep work blocks you do on a daily, weekly, and monthly basis is also important. As Brendon Burchard points out in *High Performance Habits*, spending over 50 percent of your work time producing your mission-maximizing output is game changing. Wherever you are starting from, even if it is 1 percent of your time, there is tremendous power in daily compound interest as you focus more of your time and energy on producing the work that truly moves the needle. To dig deeper on all this and dial in your approach to dropping into a maximally productive flow state, check out the related worksheet on the book's website.

If you are gearing up your personal development journey and still working on your first three pillars, then the first step of your daily productivity routine is to have a meeting with your future self. Start the day with a focused session working on your purpose, your priority, and your power plant. Following the tenets of habit formation, commit to do this seven days a week (or at least every weekday) such that there's no debate with yourself about whether to do it or not on any given day. Set the duration of this personal planning session to whatever length you are sure you can handle, even on your least-energized days. Don't be afraid to start small. Those who are afraid to start small never get the chance to truly play big. If what you can consistently commit to is just a sixty-second meeting with your future self each morning, that's okay. Use this time to ask yourself a focusing question, like: *At the end of this day, what must be true for me to feel like I've lived in alignment with my best self and made the biggest contribution I could?* At the book's website, you can find a link to the digital planner page I use each day for this meeting with myself.

Pillar 5: Positive Presence

Positive presence is about being in a resourceful state of mind in which you are able to focus on meeting other people's needs, not just your own. Positive presence is about empathy and connection with others. Remember the third commitment of joyful impact? Positive presence is about treating others with consideration, not contempt.

There are three interrelated tools to share here:

Patch Your Potholes

If you are looking to elevate your positive presence with others, a great starting point is finding and fixing your most damaging patterns of negative presence. All of us have done or said things in the moment that we later regret. This is part of being human—we all make mistakes. Yet many of us repeatedly fall into the same psychological potholes. This follows a well-established pattern: every time a predictable external event occurs, it triggers us into a snap reaction that we later regret because it does damage to ourselves and to others.

This is the Reaction/Regret Cycle. Making mistakes may be inevitable, but getting stuck in a cycle like this is not. The good news is that not only can we break this cycle, but we can actually condition ourselves to replace that snap reaction with a more thoughtful action that better serves us. We can create an Action/Alignment Cycle where our actions fully support our values and express our highest and best selves. The following questions help you understand where your immediate reaction is coming from, appreciate how there are actually positive intentions behind it, and identify an alternative course of action to take moving forward.

- What is a repeated external event that has reliably triggered you into an immediate reaction you later regretted?
- What physical sensations and emotions did you experience when you were reacting?
- What was the positive intention behind your reaction? Which of your seven instinctive drives was this reaction trying to help you meet? Hint: look at your four lower-level, self-preserving drives (security, social status, social connection, and novelty/adventure). What were you afraid of losing or of not being able to do or to have in that moment when you reacted?
- What would you have to believe was true about how the world worked and what it would take to meet your needs for your reaction to make perfect sense? Do you believe those things now, as you're looking back on this situation with the benefit of hindsight?
- What would you need to do to turn that belief into an assumption you could test out in a way that felt safe and even fun?
- Now, take a step back. Remember that the only thing any of us has to work with from one moment to the next is our own thoughts, feelings, and actions. Therefore, what

do you really want for yourself in this situation? What are the feelings you want to have? What are the feelings you don't want to have? What actions are aligned with what you value most?

- Keep in mind what's really most important to you in this whole situation. If you had all the time in the world to choose a thoughtful response each time this situation came up in the future, what alternative action would you want to take moving forward?

- Are there any larger systems at play that keep setting you up to fall into the Reaction/Regret Cycle? What can you do to reengineer these circumstances and step outside these systems?

Listen Deeply

This is about bringing genuine interest and empathetic connection to others whenever you can. We talked about this in Chapter 10. Many of us are uncomfortable with listening deeply to ourselves, let alone others. One reason deep listening is uncomfortable is that it opens us up to the possibility that we will be moved by what we hear. When the issue at hand is something deeply entwined with our own identity, we have an instinct to protect ourselves from this threat. Brain scan research has shown that when people engage with others who have deeply opposing views, our most primitive fight-or-flight circuits light up like a Christmas tree.

Challenging as it may be, we're at a point in human history where we've never been more in need of deep listening. Our differences feel profound, and not every divide can or should be bridged. But what might you come to understand if you gave yourself—and others—the gift of deep, compassionate listening?

Cultivate the practice of powerful conversations

There are two fundamental rules for a powerful conversation. First, your orientation is to serve the other person and the larger whole you are both a part of as deeply as you can. You do this both by exercising your practice of deep listening and by looking around your world for whatever can best help you both move forward in pursuit of *their* fullest self and calling for service.

Second, even though your focus is not on getting something for yourself, don't neglect to share what you are most passionately pursuing and whatever is most challenging for you in pursuit of this calling. This step is vital for opening up to the fullest possibilities of advancing what is bigger than both of you. It is this mutual sharing that gives the conversation its deepest power.

Something magical can happen in a powerful conversation. You both can't wait to continue it. You find ways to advance each other's mission, and you uncover shared interests in ways you could never have anticipated beforehand.

Here are two straightforward questions you can both ask and answer to bring your fullest positive presence to a conversation and make it as powerful as it can be:

- What would make this next year (or day, week, or month) extraordinary for you?
- What is the single greatest challenge standing between you and that extraordinary vision?

Rest assured, when you show up in conversations with such a powerfully positive presence, you and the other person—and the world at large—will experience returns beyond your imagining.

Pillar 6: Persistent Courage

Stepping up your courage is all about resetting your survival instinct circuit breaker. We are all wired for progress and growth—it's a fundamental part of our humanity. We have these higher-level needs for evolving and transcending and for contributing to the greater good. This book is written for all of us who feel a particularly strong drive to contribute and to make the world a better place. But here's the thing: these higher-level needs are in a dynamic dance with our ego-driven needs. The journey of joyful impact is about getting your psychology aligned around growing. Stretching yourself is essential to maximize your contribution to the greater good and your connection to that which is larger than yourself.

The challenge is that we don't usually start out in such clear alignment with our calling. And anytime *anything* interferes with your ability to meet your lower-level egocentric needs for security, social connection, status, and novelty, your circuit breaker gets tripped. It cuts power to the circuit that your primitive brain sees as a threat. If your sense of purpose is pulling you to grow in ways that would require even a minor change to your core routines, you may very often find yourself inexplicably immobilized, with no power to move forward despite your clear and sustained intention to do so.

For example, for several years after I started my own journey of self-development, I had clarity that I really wanted to write a book, start a blog, and generally share what I was learning more broadly. I had full certainty that stepping up my game as a thought leader would be one of the most impactful contributions I could make. Accordingly, I set aside hours of time in my calendar every week with work blocks dedicated to writing. But when I got to these places in my calendar, I would find myself doing anything except actually writing! What was going on? Why couldn't I get myself to write even though I had so much clarity and intention about doing so? The answer is that my unspoken, fearful beliefs about what would happen if I did move forward as a thought leader were tripping my survival instinct circuit breaker. My system's fight-or-flight brain was activated every time I got anywhere close to following through on my writing intention.

Robert Kegan and Lisa Lahey wrote an excellent book about this in 2009 called *Immunity to Change*. The metaphor they use is that we have an immune system that protects us from moving outside of our psychological comfort zone. Their book offers an exercise called "Immunity Mapping," and that inspired me to adapt and add to this framework to create the tool I'm sharing here. The idea is that by mapping your circuitry in more detail, you can understand what particular fears are tripping your circuit breaker. This allows you to take concrete action to safely test those fears and set aside the fears that aren't actually well-founded.

Here's what this looks like:

- Name your *one* big thing. What is a key priority, personally or professionally, that you need and want to take action on more consistently, such that if you could just get yourself to do it, you would unlock a cascade of other benefits?
- Identify all the things you do instead of the one big thing. Keep a journal if you need to over time, but simply recalling them and making a comprehensive list is a great basis for this exercise. *It should be painful to make this list.* You're on the right track if you feel yourself cringing as you take this inventory of all the ways you do *anything* but the *one thing* you've identified as truly being the most important.
- Now, what are you afraid would happen if you ceased the replacement behaviors and started doing the *one* thing? Brainstorm all the bad things you are afraid would happen.
- Once you've named your fears, a useful way to get deeper insight is to connect each of these fears with a particular kind of pain. That's because we can think of fear as anticipated pain. Therefore, it stands to reason that we can

reduce fear by reducing how painful something will be if it happens and/or reducing the likelihood that it will happen. Often, we get caught in a loop between our thoughts and our feelings, and this paralyzes us from action. This is the circuit breaker we've been talking about. The simplest way to manage your fear is to try to convince yourself that the anticipated pain isn't going to happen. The most immediate way to do that is to stop doing the things that take you down the road that leads to this painful future. That's your circuit breaker tripping you up and shutting off the power to pursue your dreams.

So, how do you get your circuit breaker to stop firing off on a hair trigger? By changing the way you evaluate pain itself and by making other shifts to lessen the severity of the anticipated pain. The more keyed up we get thinking about the potential for pain in the future, the more pain we actually experience in the moment—our primitive brains are wired like that. Brendon Burchard's 2012 book *The Charge* has a useful typology for three categories of pain: pain of loss, process pain, and outcome pain.

- **Pain of loss** is just what it sounds like. This is the discomfort you experience when you no longer have something you value. You can experience the pain of loss simply by anticipating that you'll lose access to something before it even happens. Simply imagining a future without a loved one is painful to contemplate, for instance.

- **Process pain** is the discomfort you experience when doing something difficult like running a marathon or writing a term paper. Just imagining what it will feel like to do something difficult is often enough to activate your body's fight-or-flight circuitry. This dumps adrenaline and other chemicals into your bloodstream and makes you feel that sensation of butterflies in the pit of your stomach.
- **Outcome pain** is the disappointment you feel when the result of your efforts is not what you hoped for. For example, when you trained to run that marathon for months but dropped out halfway through with blisters. Another example would be receiving a C+ on your term paper even after working on it for weeks.

After mapping each of your fears to one of these three kinds of pain, let's look at how you can take the bite out of these fears.

Counteracting Pain of Loss

If you are afraid of losing something, what have you been doing to protect yourself from the possibility of this loss? What are your options to defuse this fear?

- **Get creative**: What other alternatives do you have for acquiring or achieving this thing you'd lose? This can be especially helpful if the thing you are afraid of losing is a vehicle you are currently using to meet your egocentric or higher-level human needs.

- **Get realistic**: Test out how likely it is that you will actually lose the thing you're afraid of losing. Find a way to make these tests both fun and revealing. It can be reassuring to realize you have been overly pessimistic in calculating the odds.
- **Get stoic**: What if you lost *all* of that? How bad would that really be?

Counteracting Process Pain

If you are afraid of going through a painful process, what are your options to defuse this fear?

- **Prepare**: Plan, train, and engineer the process to optimize it. Remember that marathon? Get shoes that fit and special anti-blister socks, and pack some carbohydrate gel to keep from bonking.
- **Elevate your motivation**: Get fired up about how much you want what's on the other side, even if it will be painful to get there.
- **Rewire yourself**: Attribute a different meaning to the experience. "I'm not anxious; I'm excited." You'll feel the same butterflies in your stomach, but in a different way.
- **Desensitize yourself**: Repeated small-dose exposures can minimize your anxious reaction. For example, a great way to get past writer's block is to commit to write just two hundred words each day, no matter what. You can

most often do this in twenty minutes or less—and if you get in the groove, you can just keep going!

Counteracting Outcome Pain

If you are afraid of a disappointing outcome, what are your options to defuse this fear?

- **Prepare:** Plan, train, and do whatever else you can to increase your odds of a favorable outcome.
- **Rinse and repeat:** Remind yourself that the best way to succeed is to try, learn, and try again. Operate on the premise that you will keep trying until you get the outcome you're after. In effect, associate the pain of disappointment with getting closer to your goal. Falling short isn't painful; it's all about making progress and momentum.
- **Reconcile:** Orient yourself to appreciate the value in the experience, whatever the outcome.

Now, how can you test whether the pain you fear is actually real? It's time to playfully and safely experiment with what actually happens when you tweak these rules. For example, when I used this process for myself, my *one* thing was stepping out as a thought leader, which of course includes writing this book. As I mapped out the fears that were getting in my way, I realized I was anticipating pain of loss around losing clients if I expressed myself freely. This was manifest in the fact that I had an unspoken rule for myself that I would never set foot inside a particular client's office without wearing a suit. I decided to play with that fear by one day wearing some sneakers with my suit. Lo and behold, that was the day when I first noticed how half the people in that office were also wearing sneakers. I haven't felt like I had to wear a suit with that client ever since. More importantly, I've felt more comfortable offering my perspective even when it runs against the grain—which has helped me create that much more value as an advisor.

There is tremendous power in harnessing your subconscious to overcome fears. This is the world of directive affirmations. It's important to tell yourself you're already doing the thing you fear, and it's important to take stock of the benefits you are experiencing as a result. When you speak to yourself every day out loud and with conviction, you are training your subconscious that this behavior is not just safe but profoundly attractive. Instead of standing in your way and firing the circuit breaker every time you get near something challenging, your subconscious mind will start going to work in service of your aspirations. There is a powerful principle in play here called *reticular activation*. We often experience this in our lives as serendipity. Just as I needed something, there it was coming into my life in abundance. When you activate your subconscious as an ally in your growth, it is able to parse through many more signals from the outside world than your conscious mind can. Your primitive fight-or-flight brain is primed to process every single iota of information your sensory systems can physically perceive. Most of this signal traffic never makes it to your conscious mind. You'd be totally overwhelmed if it did! But imagine if the same mental circuitry that spots threats was also primed to spot incoming opportunities for advancing your greatest dreams and aspirations. Who wouldn't want that working for them?

Pillar 7: Expanded Perspective

Your greatest contribution as a change agent rests on being able to transcend yourself. This is about looking past your own concerns to perceive the bigger system around you. Being able to see the complex world around you with a critical yet appreciative eye is vital to *getting real* about how change actually plays out in the world. Doing your best to see past your own blind spots and biases is also critical to understanding your own role in the systems you seek to change. With this clarity, you can begin to help others do the same.

Let's take a closer look at three ways to expand your perspective that are particularly helpful when it comes to gearing up for meaningful giving.

Three Tools for Expanding Your Perspective

1. *Tuning In to Your State of Mind*

The graphic below lays out a framework for five different states of mind and how these influence our self-orientation—how we go about meeting our fundamental needs. As we discussed in Chapter 11, we all move between different states of mind, sometimes from one moment to the next. Getting better at recognizing which of these states of mind you are in at any given moment is a great start to expanding your perspective. This is particularly true when you realize that each state of mind has a lot to do with what you will notice and how you will focus your energy in that moment.

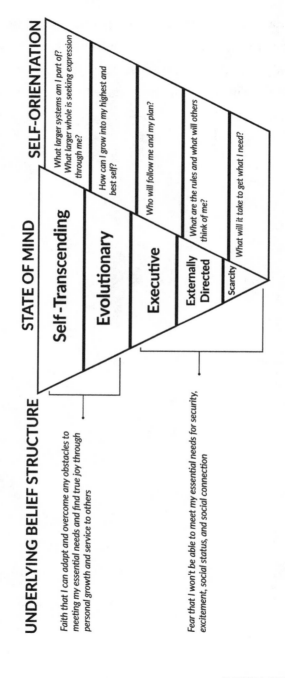

2. Connecting Your State of Mind to How You Show Up as a Change Agent

A second key tool for expanding your perspective is to explore how your state of mind in the moment is connected to how you engage systemic inequality and bias. This is particularly important when looking at issues of equity and identity. Download the worksheet from the book's website to explore opportunities to level up your work as a change agent by shifting your state of mind.

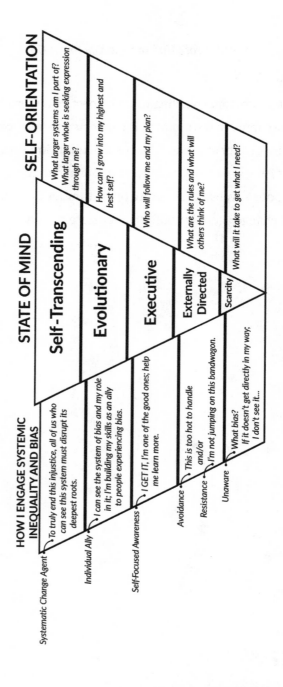

3. Tips for Taming Your Cognitive Biases

We all suffer from blind spots and cognitive biases. Sometimes, one of the most powerful things you can do to expand your perspective is simply to become more aware of what you are missing. If greater awareness is a key first step, actually curing yourself of cognitive biases is notoriously difficult. Nevertheless, there are some things you can do to reduce your susceptibility to tunnel vision and faulty reasoning.

- **Take more time.** If you have the opportunity to make a conscious choice, you very likely have enough time to actually engage in a careful reasoning process.
- **Never make a choice between only two options.** Force yourself to generate at least four possible courses of action before making a choice.
- **Make multiple estimates**. If you have to make a guess at a critical piece of data for decision-making, make several separate estimates and average them together.
- **Imagine that all your available options are suddenly gone.** What new option would you have to consider then?
- **Use pre-mortems.** This is an exercise to help you work through and solve for the possible things that could go wrong based on your chosen course of action *before* you are irrevocably committed to that course of action.
- **Use scenario planning to kill the official future.** Force yourself to consider multiple future scenarios, not just the version of the future you hope will come true.

- **Use checklists and "blind tastings" for due diligence.**
  This is vital for decisions where you know you have an
  emotional attachment or psychological need at stake.

PUTTING ALL SEVEN PILLARS INTO PRACTICE

The Seven Pillars of Personal Development will help you stretch
the boundaries of your comfort zone. Pushing through this barrier
can bring you a clearer, more powerful sense of where you may
want to step up your game. When we set our intention to grow
and surpass our fears, we open up the possibility of changing the
world for real, beginning with ourselves.

LEVELS OF PHILANTHROPIC LEADERSHIP

Identifying Your Style

"The key to successful leadership is influence, not authority."

—KEN BLANCHARD

The world has never been more in need of meaningful giving. There is no shortage of challenges worth tackling or social entrepreneurs worth supporting, yet hundreds of billions of dollars are still sitting on the sidelines. One of the most leveraged things you can do with your own giving is to influence others to give more and better. As you rise to this challenge, there are five levels of leadership for the field. In which of these ways are you called to be a leader? What larger contribution is trying to happen *through* you and your philanthropy?

1. EXEMPLAR/PRACTITIONER

This is about walking the walk as an exemplar of good practice in the field of philanthropy. It could be that your main goal is simply to do your own giving well. Perhaps you have never had any conscious aspiration to lead the field. Here's the good news: doing your own giving with joy and impact is an important act of leadership, period. You are part of the system, and what you do changes the system, by definition. Showing up as a quiet exemplar is a great contribution in itself.

2. THOUGHT LEADER

The next step beyond serving as an exemplar is to play the role of thought leader. This is about sharing what you are doing and learning through your giving in a deliberate way. Not everyone feels like they have the time or comfort to do this. However, if you feel called to this level of leadership, here are several options for you.

First, you can help others save time, give more, and give better by making your portfolio an open book. This can be especially helpful if you have made a large investment in diligence and sourcing. You don't need to keep the secret of your success locked away in a vault. Quite the opposite. In the philanthropic space, if you've found a path to giving with joy and impact, there's little reason not to share your full roadmap.

It's also important to have a frank and open discussion of what hasn't worked. We don't see enough of this in philanthropy. One reason is that donors don't want to do even more damage to the grantees they are stepping away from. Why add insult to injury by making it harder for them to raise money from other funders as well? But what if you had a different view of what's at stake? Let's imagine a house on fire where you discover the main stairway is blocked by a fallen ceiling. You would let everyone else know so others could focus their life-saving efforts on a different path. You would also help anyone still inside the house who needed to find a better way out.

Finally, share your questions. Don't be afraid to make clear the active edge of your own learning as a philanthropist.

3. CONVENER

Creating spaces in which donors can learn from each other, grantees, and others on the front lines can be an incredibly valuable leadership contribution to the field. One reason the pace of cultural change in philanthropy is so slow is that the work is often carried out in isolation. This was certainly a key reason Bill and Melinda Gates and Warren Buffett joined forces in 2010 to launch the Giving Pledge, a voluntary movement in which high-capacity donors publicly express their commitment to give away at least half their wealth. The Giving Pledge also creates a space to convene its members in a learning community of peers that is professionally staffed and supported. Likewise, Schmidt Futures has played a leading role by convening a community of philanthropy advisors through the P150 initiative, building on the insight that a great way to help other high-capacity donors gear up their giving is to better equip and interconnect the people who advise them.

You, too, can take action to shift the culture of philanthropy in your own way. Gathering even a handful of folks to explore what you are learning makes a difference. If in-person gatherings aren't your thing, virtual convening has lots of value too. What if you interviewed one of your outstanding grantees and shared this with other donors?

As you bring others together, be aware that creating pitch-free zones can be important. Often, other donors don't want to get overwhelmed with asks. Find ways to bring people together on their own terms and on a nontransactional basis.

4. TRUSTED ADVISOR AND COACH

Another level of field leadership is coaching and advising. This is where you show up as a trusted advisor to fellow philanthropists. What does it take to be a trusted advisor? Let's run through the list of attributes.

Trusted advisors:

- Keep visionary social impact as the North Star for themselves and those they advise.

- Focus on the needs of those they advise, not their own needs.
- Help other donors realize their highest selves through their giving.
- Help those they advise find positive outlets to meet lower-level needs.
- Refrain from relying on the advising relationship to meet their own lower-level needs for security, excitement, status, and connection.
- Seek and speak the truth to everyone, including their advisees and themselves.
- Seek understanding and solutions from those closest to the issues at hand.
- Acknowledge the limits of their own knowledge, skills, and mindset and search out their own blind spots and biases.
- Provide course corrections that are both empathetic and unfailing.
- Treat those they advise and everyone else with consideration, not contempt.
- Engage collaboratively with other donors and practitioners about their ideas and remain open to being influenced by the ideas of others.
- Use persuasion and inspiration when appropriate, but never pressure tactics of manipulation.
- Show up as encouraging coaches in their advisee's corner, believing in that person's potential for meaningful giving even when the advisee might not.

- Provide options to choose from, not answers to install.

If this path is appealing to you, here are some further suggestions for how to elevate your qualities as a trusted advisor:

- Commit to the daily pursuit of personal growth (and joy!) across all areas of your own life.
- Be part of mastermind groups.
- Understand, evolve, and elevate your own psychology.
- Get serious about the fundamentals of your own wellness: sleep, nutrition, movement, and mindfulness.
- Work with a coach yourself. The further you go in your own journey of growth, the more you can propel others.
- Get trained as a coach.

While there are certainly preparations you can make to lean into the role of advisor and coach, don't be afraid to simply *get started*. You can add tremendous value in this role without being an expert or a perfect exemplar. You simply need to be open to listening deeply and sharing your own experience frankly. Despite the name, one of the most effective ways to build trust as an advisor is *not* to give advice. Instead, share your experience. You rarely know enough about someone else's specific circumstances to give them advice that truly fits. It is far more valuable to share the most relevant aspects of your own experience. Afterward, the advisee can decide how best to apply that experience in their own context.

5. TRANSCENDENT POWER SHIFTER AND SYSTEMIC CHANGE AGENT

The next level up as field leader is to transcend yourself completely. This is about showing up in ways that shift power and promote systemic change on the issues that matter most. This is what you do when you focus on helping others take their own leadership to the highest possible level. You support others to exert profound agency in their own ways over the systems that have held them back. This is where restorative philanthropy or philanthropy as reparations comes from. It isn't even remotely about you when you are in this stage of field leadership. Many people may never even know about the profundity of your contribution. Consider Emil Schwarzhaupt and the foundation he left as a legacy to carry out their mission in the twenty-five years after his death in the early 1950s. The foundation's leadership set aside ego to work behind the scenes on building leadership in others. In the process, they made profound contributions to the movement-building infrastructure of the Civil Rights Movement—from the United Farm Workers to Saul Alinsky to the Highlander Folk School and the Freedom Riders.

When you have transcended yourself, you truly make the greatest possible impact on systemic change. Along the way, you are very likely to find deep joy in elevating others and helping them actualize their own potential. If there's an ultimate meaning to life, perhaps this is it: to grow into your own full potential to better help others reach theirs. To say it even more simply, the meaning of life is a life of meaning.

To what level of leadership in the field do you aspire? The five levels we've looked at here are not necessarily a sequential progression. Whatever level feels like the right fit for you now, I urge you to reach at least one level beyond that comfort zone. This is how, together, we can truly accelerate change in a field that so desperately needs reinvention and reinvigoration. Change starts with you, and that change starts from within. As you gear up your giving and commit to change the world for real, remember that it begins with the person in the mirror.

CONCLUSION

Where We Are and What Comes Next

"Give yourself a gift: the present moment."

—MARCUS AURELIUS

Seventy years ago, Emil Schwarzhaupt helped shape the course of American history with just $4 million. This is how much money his foundation spent to aid the Civil Rights Movement and other citizen-led community movements in the twenty-five years following his death in 1950. One of the Schwarzhaupt Foundation's first major grantees was the Highlander Folk School. A key feature of their grant support was that it was open-ended. It was designed to allow the organization to experiment and develop unproven ideas. Just a few years later, Martin Luther King Jr, Rosa Parks, John Lewis, and other leading lights of the Civil Rights Movement came to Highlander Folk School for training in nonviolent organizing. It was from there that "We Shall Overcome"—the iconic anthem of the movement—spread across the country and around the globe. Another major grantee of the foundation was Cesar Chavez and the United Farm Workers, as well as Saul Alinsky and the

Industrial Areas Foundation, who have taught and trained count-less community organizers across the country in the decades since.

It took Emil Schwarzhaupt the entire first half of the twenti-eth century to accumulate his philanthropic legacy of $4 million. When Forbes released its 2021 list of billionaires in the throes of a global pandemic, there were a record-breaking *ninety-eight* newly minted billionaires from the United States in that single year alone. These first-time billionaires have a combined net worth of almost $250 billion. They join 626 fellow Americans already on the list—and let's not look only at the billionaires. Add it all up, and we've got 101,000 families in the United States with at least $30 million in net worth each, at a combined total of at least $11.2 trillion.[24] Collectively, these folks are giving away about .75 percent of this wealth each year.[25]

There is a *tremendous* amount of potential good that wealthy Americans can participate in with their increasing resources. And yes, a tremendous amount of this money is still sitting on the sidelines while the world's problems get more complex than ever. But you already know that these aggregate numbers aren't the most interesting or actionable part of the story.

You want to be part of the solution, and ultimately, the most important questions are the ones you must ask yourself. What kind of impact can you have with your giving? What meaning and fulfillment can philanthropy bring to you and your family? How can you gear up for giving that truly makes sense for the world and for you? With this book, you should be more prepared to both ask and act on these important questions.

So, what should you do now? Put these tools and techniques into use in your own giving! Visit the book's website (moneywith meaningbook.co) and take advantage of the resources available there, including videos, worksheets, and additional material to draw on in your journey.

Figure out the most meaningful path for you, and determine what kind of giving brings the most impact and the most joy for you, your family, and the universe of social entrepreneurs engaged on the issues you care about. Become an ambassador of this approach to philanthropy. Whatever level of leadership you already aspire to in your giving, push yourself to take at least one step beyond your comfort zone. By operating in this way and elevating joy as well as impact through your giving, you'll be helping to shift the culture of philanthropy in a profoundly positive way.

Imagine a movement of people committed to the four principles of joyful impact in philanthropy:

1. Get Visionary: Prioritize visionary social impact above ego-driven needs.
2. Get Real: Seek and speak the truth to everyone, including yourself.
3. Get Together: Treat others with consideration, not contempt.
4. Get Better: Commit to the daily practice of personal development, learning, and growth.

Step forward to be part of this growing community of donors, advisors, and change agents who are all committed to grappling with the peril and promise of our world's key challenges. The work begins within each of them, just as it begins within you. The world can't wait for more meaningful philanthropy—giving that brings impact *and* joy. The world needs you and the good your philanthropy can bring.

It all starts with you. The moment is now. Your money matters, and you can give it lasting meaning. You can change the world for real.

ACKNOWLEDGMENTS

It's been a long journey from idea to author, and this book wouldn't be here without the support of many along the way! I'd like to express my thanks and recognition to some of you here.

For my wife, Caroline: I cherish your love and partnership in our life's journey and have deeply appreciated your wise counsel at key points in the writing process.

For my partners and colleagues at Building Impact: I am grateful for your support and encouragement on so many levels and for the opportunity to be part of such a committed team taking action every day to make the world a better place. A special thanks to the remarkable Brenda Calderon. You have been an incredibly thoughtful and wise-beyond-your years colleague in all things Joyful Impact for the past three years! Thanks as well to Jhaya Apas. I am grateful for all the ways you have helped make the creative process easier, including your help producing the weekly blog that I have used to work out many of the ideas in this book.

Many thanks as well to the team at Scribe Media. There's a book just waiting to be written inside so many of us, and you have made my author's journey possible. I especially want to thank Eliece Poole for guiding me so well through each step of the publishing process, Jennifer Glover for your patience and care editing the manuscript, and Jess LaGreca for your creative design talents.

I also want to acknowledge and remember the support of my mother, Cheryl Johnston, who did not live to see this book completed. As a lifelong educator, you taught me and so many of your students how to think critically and how to write. I am grateful that you had a chance to read early drafts and grace the margins with comments in that familiar green pen!

I am grateful to the participants in the Joyful Impact Accelerator for social entrepreneurs. Each of you has such a compelling vision for a better world and is taking action every day, often against the odds, to bring that vision into reality. You show all of us engaged in philanthropy that when we get behind visionary leaders with proximity and passion for solving real-world challenges, joy and impact abound!

I also want to thank the participants of our Advisors Accelerator program. You have given me invaluable insight and wisdom about how philanthropy can be different and better from your unique perspective as trusted advisors to an array of donors. An extra thanks to those of you whose close reading of early drafts helped me spot missing pieces and add important content.

Lastly, I want to thank all the individual donors and foundation staff I have had the opportunity to advise (and in some cases coach) over the past decade. It has been a privilege to strive and learn alongside you as you have turned your time, talents, and resources of all kinds into meaningful giving.

REFERENCES AND RESOURCES

Easy-to-click links to the books, studies, and organizations mentioned in *Money with Meaning* can be found on the book's website: www.moneywithmeaningbook.co

The book's website also features instructional videos and downloadable worksheets to accompany many sections of the book.

ABOUT THE AUTHOR

Alex Johnston is the president and founder of Building Impact, a philanthropic advising practice that has helped its clients distribute more than $750 million over ten years. He is also a Certified High Performance Coach and has worked with dozens of donors, philanthropy advisors, and social entrepreneurs seeking more impact and more joy across their lives. Alex is a member of the Entrepreneurs Organization and serves on a number of nonprofit boards including FaithACTs for Education and the Trust for Learning. He lives in New York City, New York, and New Haven, Connecticut, with his wife, Caroline, and their three sons.

ENDNOTES

1 Albrecht, L. (2020, August 10). *The giving pledge turns 10: These billionaires pledged to give away half their wealth, but they soon ran into a problem.* MarketWatch. https://www.marketwatch.com/story/giving-away-money -well-is-very-hard-the-giving-pledge-turns-10-and-its-signers-are-richer -than-ever-2020-08-08. Data on annual giving is from *The Chronicle of Philanthropy*'s annual report: Di Mento, M. (2022, February 8). *The philan-thropy 50.* The Chronicle of Philanthropy. https://www.philanthropy.com /article/the-philanthropy-50/#id=browse_2021.

2 Federal Trade Commission. (2019, March 28). *FTC, states continue fight against sham charities; shut down operations that falsely claimed to help dis-abled police officers and veterans* [Press release]. https://www.ftc.gov/news -events/news/press-releases/2019/03/ftc-states-continue-fight-against -sham-charities-shut-down-operations-falsely-claimed-help-disabled.

3 You can find this online assessment at https://www.culturalevolution.org /worldview-questionnaire/

4 Imberg, M., Shaban, M., & Warburton, S. (2021) *Wealth-X: World ultra wealth report 2021.* Wealth-X. https://go.wealthx.com/world-ultra-wealth -report-2021.

5 Berger, A. (2021, November 22). *2021 allocation to GiveWell top charities: Why we're giving more going forward.* Good Ventures. *Give & Learn Blog.*

https://www.goodventures.org/blog/2021-allocation-givewell-top-charities
-why-were-giving-more-going-forward.

6 Davis, A., & Pearl, M. (2021, July 14). *Billionaires say they can't give their
money away fast enough. Nonprofit Quarterly.* https://nonprofitquarterly.org
/billionaires-say-they-cant-give-their-money-away-fast-enough-heres-how/.

7 Brest, P. (2015). *Strategic philanthropy and its discontents. Stanford Social
Innovation Review.* https://doi.org/10.48558/EA5M-4C07.

8 For a thought-provoking treatment of these three kinds of problems, see:
Glouberman, S., & Zimmerman, B. (2002). *Complicated and complex systems:
What would successful reform of Medicare look like?* (Discussion Paper No. 8)
Commission on the Future of Health Care in Canada. https://www.alnap
.org/system/files/content/resource/files/main/complicatedandcomplex
systems-zimmermanreport-medicare-reform.pdf.

9 *Keep refining: Peter Lynch says becoming effective in philanthropy requires trial
and error.* (2013, November 27). The Bridgespan Group. Retrieved May 22,
2022, from https://www.bridgespan.org/insights/library/remarkable-givers
/profiles/peter-and-carolyn-lynch/keep-refining%E2%80%9D-peter-lynch
-says-becoming-effecti.

10 *Creative approach to disease research pays off.* (n.d.) The Philanthropy Round-
table. Retrieved May 22, 2022, from https://www.philanthropyroundtable
.org/resource/creative-approach-to-disease-research-pays-off./

11 Wadman, M. (2021, April 23). *Malaria vaccine has striking early success after
decades of disappointment. Science.* https://www.science.org/content/article
/malaria-vaccine-has-striking-early-success-after-decades-disappointment.

12 Morgan Stanley Institute for Sustainable Investing. (2019). *Sustainable
reality: Analyzing the risks and returns of sustainable funds* [White paper].

Morgan Stanley. https://www.morganstanley.com/content/dam/msdotcom
/ideas/sustainable-investing-offers-financial-performance-lowered-risk
/Sustainable_Reality_Analyzing_Risk_and_Returns_of_Sustainable
_Funds.pdf.

13 See https://pacscenter.stanford.edu/about/

14 Sun, L. H., & Brittain, A. (2019, June 19). *Meet the New York couple donating
millions to the anti-vax movement. Washington Post.* https://www.washington
post.com/national/health-science/meet-the-new-york-couple-donating
-millions-to-the-anti-vax-movement/2019/06/18/9d791bcc-8e28-11e9
-b08e-cfd89bd36d4e_story.html.

15 Jones, B. L., & Unsworth, R. K. F. (2020). *The perverse fisheries consequences
of mosquito net malaria prophylaxis in East Africa. Ambio 49,* 1257–1267.
https://doi.org/10.1007/s13280-019-01280-0.

16 This approach to root cause analysis draws inspiration in part from a
paper presented by Jack Harich: Harich, J., Bangerter, P., & Durlacher, S.
(2012, July 31–August 4). *Solving the sustainability crisis with root cause analysis* [Paper presentation]. Ecosystem Services Partnership Conference,
Portland, OR, United States. https://www.thwink.org/sustain/publications
/papers/Harich_2012_SolvingSusProblemWithRCA.pdf.

17 *Defining critical thinking.* (n.d.). The Foundation for Critical Thinking.
Retrieved July 9, 2022, from https://www.criticalthinking.org/pages
/defining-critical-thinking/766.

18 McKenzie, C. R. M. (2004). Framing effects in inference tasks and why
they're normatively defensible. *Memory & Cognition, 32,* 874–885.
https://doi.org/10.3758/BF03196866.

19 Broekhoff, D., Gillenwater, M., Colbert-Sangre, T. & Cage, P. (2019). *Securing climate benefit: A guide to using carbon offsets.* Stockholm

Environment Institute and Greenhouse Gas Management Institute.
http://www.offsetguide.org/wp-content/uploads/2020/03/Carbon
-Offset-Guide_3122020.pdf.

20 Glouberman, S., & Zimmerman, B. (2002). *Complicated and complex systems: What would successful reform of Medicare look like?* (Discussion Paper No. 8) Commission on the Future of Health Care in Canada. https://www.alnap.org/system/files/content/resource/files/main /complicatedandcomplexsystems-zimmermanreport-medicare -reform.pdf.

21 Hearn, S., & Buffardi, A. (2016, February 15). *What is impact?* [Working paper]. Overseas Development Institute. https://odi.org/en/publications /what-is-impact/.

22 Steve Teles and Mark Schmitt have an excellent article making this case in the *Stanford Social Innovation Review*: Teles, S., & Schmitt, M. (2011). *The elusive craft of evaluating advocacy. Stanford Social Innovation Review*, 9(3), 38–43. https://doi.org/10.48558/Y90Q-VE61.

23 Bekkers, R. (2018). *Stability, reliability and validity of social value orientation*. OSF. https://osf.io/5emfp/.

24 Imberg, M., Shaban, M. & Warburton, S. (2021). *World Ultra Wealth Report 2021*. Wealth X. https://go.wealthx.com/world-ultra-wealth-report-2021.

25 Imberg, M. & Shaban, M. (2022). *Ultra High Net Worth Philanthropy 2022*. Wealth X. https://go.wealthx.com/download-ultra-high-net-worth -philanthropy-report-2022.

Printed in the USA
CPSIA information can be obtained
at www.ICGtesting.com
LVHW041743131223
766027LV00031B/693/J